TERRINE DE BODY...

RAISED PORK PIE...

VEAL & BACON LOAF...

STUFFED TOMATOES...

HAM & CLAM LOAF...

PÂTÉ DE CAMPAGNE...

PORK & SPINACH LOAF...

VEAL, PORK & LIVER LOAF...

...WITH CREAMED ONIONS

Pâtés &

Other Marvelous

Meat Loaves

Books by Dorothy Ivens

Cookbooks
Pâtés & Other Marvelous Meat Loaves
Pasta Pronto! (with William E. Massee)
Glorious Stew

Children's Books
The Upside-Down Boy
Bozy and All the Children
The Long Hike

Pâtés &
Other Marvelous
Meat Loaves

by DOROTHY IVENS

Illustrated by the author

J. B. LIPPINCOTT COMPANY
Philadelphia / New York

U.S. Library of Congress Cataloging in Publication Data

Ivens, Dorothy.
    Pâtés & other marvelous meat loaves.

    1. Cookery (Meat)   I. Title.
TX749.I93   641.8′2   72-745
ISBN-0-397-00795-7

Adaptation of "A Restricted Veal Loaf" from *The Alice B.
Toklas Cook Book* by Alice B. Toklas. Copyright, 1954, by
Alice B. Toklas. Reprinted by permission of Harper & Row,
Publishers, Inc.

Adaptation of "Tuna Pudding" from *How to Eat Better for Less
Money* by James Beard and Sam Aaron. Copyright © 1954,
1970, by James Beard and Sam Aaron. Reprinted by permission
of Simon & Schuster, Inc.

To Bill

CONTENTS

GALANTINES

HOT LOAVES

PASTRY-COVERED LOAVES

FISH LOAVES

Contents / 11

STUFFED VEGETABLES

BACK OF THE BOOK RECIPES

> A pastry recipe, a spice mixture, a few things that go particularly well with pâtés and meat loaves and the buffets built around them, and two wine punches.

VEGETABLES AND STARCHY ACCOMPANIMENTS

SALADS

COLD SAUCES

HOT SAUCES

WINE PUNCHES

INTRODUCTION

Pâtés, terrines, and galantines sound exotic and difficult to make, but basically they are just marvelous meat loaves. True, the list of ingredients may be long, and the procedure a little more complicated than simply mixing everything together. But if you can make a meat loaf, you can follow these recipes step by step to produce a variety of loaves which, whether packed into a loaf pan, stuffed into a skin, encased in pastry, or cooked and mashed into a spread, are hard to find outside of a fine restaurant.

A repertoire of cold loaves can be drawn upon for a truly dazzling number of uses, particularly if you like to entertain. Since they improve with a few days' keeping, they are there like money in the bank if they are not used up the first time around.

Pâtés and other cold loaves make marvelous first courses. Serving a first course before dinner, instead of a lot of things to eat with cocktails, is a way of life our household has come to find very agreeable. Cocktail snacks can really spoil the appetite for dinner, whereas a first course can be planned to whet the appetite rather than to kill it. A first course is also a graceful way to bring the cocktail hour to a close and makes the transition from liquor to wine an easy one. Since most cold loaves can be made as much as a week ahead, one can devote one's immediate efforts to the main course, secure in the knowledge that the refrigerator holds a glamorous beginning to the meal.

Pâtés and cold loaves can also be served as part of a cocktail or dinner buffet. Since they taste best with wine, one of the wines we suggest to go with each recipe might be offered at cocktail time as an alternative to hard drinks. Cold loaves also make a good main course at lunch or supper, and they are splendid picnic fare. We like to pack a pâté, cheese, tomatoes, some crisp raw vegetables, and fruit in a cooler—with crusty bread, wine, and stemmed wine glasses in a picnic hamper—and take off for beach or country. (Don't forget the corkscrew, carving knife, and bread knife.)

Although the book is mainly about cold loaves, it also contains some rather different and special hot loaves I have developed or discovered along the way, some of them good cold as well as hot. The category of "meat loaf" has been stretched to include Matambre and Morcon, two versions of rolled stuffed flank steak, and some fish loaves. There are also a few stuffed vegetables, related to meat loaves because of their stuffing, which are useful as main courses or as hot items for a buffet that you might build around a pâté or some other cold loaf.

Some hot loaves are also good cold, but the reverse is not true: pâtés and terrines are designed to be served cold only. They are more highly seasoned than hot loaves because coldness masks seasoning and this has to be compensated for. They are also more dense in texture, for easier slicing, and offer a lot of taste in a thin slice. So a cold loaf recipe will be different from a hot loaf recipe. Where a cold loaf will have only a little uncooked cereal, or flour, or sometimes no filler at all, a hot one is best when it is made light and tender with generous additions of a filler such as crumbled bread, and when the seasonings are not too overwhelming. Not that any hot loaf can't be served cold, but it will not be the fabulous fare that a real pâté or terrine can be, worthy of a fine wine and up to serving before the most elegant of main courses.

Equipment

Loaf pans are always measured at the top and side—length, width, and depth, in that order. When you buy a pan, volume isn't always given, but when it is, it is usually given in quarts (1 quart = 4 cups, 1¼ quarts = 5 cups, 1½ quarts = 6 cups, 2 quarts = 8 cups, etc.). Volume can be measured by filling the pan with water to the brim, then measuring the water. Ground raw meat measures 2 cups per pound. I don't know any way to measure unmarked pans in a store except to carry along a tape measure and a bag of rice or dried beans, which measure like water—4 cups to 1 quart—and either surreptitiously, or with the blessing of the store clerk, measure for yourself.

The standard 8-cup (2-quart) loaf pan is about 9 inches long, 5 inches wide, and 3 inches deep, with tiny variations from brand to brand. There is a longer, narrower version, suggested for some loaves because it makes a smaller slice. It is roughly 13 by 4½ by 2½ inches, although still holding 8 cups.

A larger pan, holding 10 cups (2½ quarts), 10 by 5 by 4 inches, is called for in the Pâté de Campagne Coach House recipe and is a more comfortable size for the Terrine de Veau et Porc. I have one I found in a restaurant supply store. It is really a steam table receptacle, made of stainless steel.

The small pan called for in many of the recipes holds 5 cups (1¼ quarts) and is about 8½ by 4½ by 2½ inches.

The pans can be stainless steel, aluminum, Pyrex, freezer-to-oven ware, enameled ironware, or nonstick silicone-lined. Tin-lined pans, though perfect for baking, will not do for loaves with much acidity —those containing a lot of lemon juice or fruit (such as apples). They can be used for pastry-covered loaves, but if you are buying new pans with pâtés and meat loaves in mind, it is better to avoid tin-lined ones.

Terrines are very handsome straight-sided ovenware dishes, and by all means use them if you have them. They come in oval and rectangular shapes, nice and deep, and usually have lids, sometimes quite fancy ones. When a recipe calls for a loaf to be covered for cooking, though, seal with foil before putting on the lid. Foil alone will make an adequate lid if it is sealed tightly. Terrines are often an in-between size—4 or 6 cups—big enough for 5- and 8-cup recipes respectively if the loaf is to be cooked uncovered and mounded. For other loaves, which have to be flattened and covered, fill the terrine to ½ inch from the top and make the excess into patties and freeze—to be cooked in the frying pan sometime for a fabulous snack, cold or hot, depending on the type of loaf it is.

The only *molds* called for in these recipes are 4-cup ones, and they can be any shape. I rather like the circular one with a hole in the middle, to fill with something pretty and edible for the serving. A 4-cup terrine or 5-cup loaf pan, of course, can be used instead.

Although it is possible to make pâtés and meat loaves without a *meat grinder* and *a kitchen scale*, they allow you much more freedom of choice and can save you money too. Leftover baked ham, for instance, can be weighed and cut up or ground as the recipe directs, or, if you buy a ham steak for the loaf, it can be weighed after trimming. Some stores are reluctant to grind meat to order, particularly pork, so with a scale and grinder you can prepare your own. Since the pork for pâtés and meat loaves is best when it has fat in it (one part fat to three parts lean, unless lean is specified), you can buy boned shoulders or shoulder chops and weigh and grind them, reserving the excess for other uses. The chops can be boned with a sharp knife; allow at least a third extra weight for bone content when you buy them, and be very careful to remove small bone splinters. Sometimes a recipe calls for lean pork and fresh pork fat, and a few loin pork chops are fine for this, with the lean and fat weighed separately after boning and either ground together or the lean ground and the fat chopped, according to the recipe. I buy stewing veal and stewing lamb—or shoulder lamb chops when they are on sale—and freeze it, to trim or bone, weigh, and grind when I need it. Stewing meat needs to be trimmed of membranes and hard gristly pieces and fat. Veal should have no fat, and lamb should have not more than one part fat to three parts lean, so buy more than the recipe calls for. Beef and pork liver can usually be chopped as an alternative to grinding, but sometimes grinding it with some other ingredients gives the loaf its particular texture.

Blenders seem to be standard equipment these days, but an alternative method is given wherever possible. Some things, like mousses, cannot be made without a blender.

Sharp *knives* are essential. You need a small pointed boning knife for your home butchering and for boning duck and chicken for galantines. You will also need a large French chef's knife of carbon steel, easily sharpened with a sharpening steel, for chopping meat, and a stainless steel chopping knife for vegetables.

Storage

Pâtés, terrines, and galantines keep well and even improve with keeping for about a week in the refrigerator. Before unmolding, the fat on the top helps to keep them fresh, but they should still be covered with foil. Once unmolded, they should be well wrapped in foil for refrigerator storage. They do not freeze well, but the raw mixtures can be frozen. Frozen raw mixtures should be defrosted before cooking, to ensure thorough cooking according to the time given in the recipe. Chicken-liver spreads and mousses do not keep as long in the refrigerator and cannot be frozen. Raw pâté and terrine mixtures should be frozen *without* the pork fat (or bacon) that lines their pan.

Weighting Cold Loaves

A very useful thing to have around for pâté-making is a brick. Many pâtés and terrines require weighting after cooking, to press out fat and to make the loaf firm for slicing. Some are cooked with a weight on them. A brick is the perfect thing; it is the right weight and size and is eminently ovenproof.

Without a brick, which weighs about 4 pounds, some improvisation will be needed. To weight a loaf *after* cooking, fill another loaf pan, the bottom of which just fits the top of the cooked loaf, with rice or dried beans or three or four 1-pound cans of food, or the equivalent in silverware or other objects. For a loaf that needs a weight *during* cooking, use the pan filled with beans or rice. If you haven't another pan, wrap 8 cups of beans or rice in heavy foil and shape to fit the top of the loaf. When a cooked loaf is close to the top of the pan, there is apt to be some overflow when it is weighted, so it is well to have another pan under it to catch the overflow.

How to Test Pork for Seasoning

Raw meat mixtures containing pork cannot be tasted because of the danger of trichinosis. Flatten a rounded teaspoonful of the well-mixed mixture and cook it in a skillet filmed with oil. If it is to be a cold loaf, cool and chill the sample before tasting.

About This Book

Each recipe is preceded by suggestions for ways to serve the loaf and for wines and other dishes that could accompany it. The back of the book contains a few recipes for vegetables, salads, and sauces that go particularly well with the loaves; it also contains a recipe for pastry that is especially good for pastry-enclosed loaves, hot or cold, a recipe for a spice mixture to make in quantity for use in several pâtés, and two wine punch recipes. When these recipes are mentioned in the text they are marked with an asterisk (*).

The "we" that occurs occasionally in the text is neither regal nor editorial. My husband, Bill Massee, author of several books on wine and food, has supplied enthusiastic help in selecting the wines and foods to go with the pâtés and meat loaves as we have tried them.

I would like to thank Philip Hall and Mary Gandall for their cheerful help and interest, which have enhanced the book and added greatly to my enjoyment in the doing of it.

DOROTHY IVENS

Cold Loaves

PÂTÉS

Pâté de Campagne
Pork, Veal, and Liver Loaf

Some French housewives may make their own pâtés because they prefer them, but they don't have to. Wherever they live, in city, town, or village, they are never far from a store called a *charcuterie* that sells a marvelous collection of pâtés, terrines, molded loaves of liver or ham, loaves in pastry, loaves in aspic, and cooked and uncooked sausages. Nostalgic travelers will remember choosing a variety of these wonders in small towns all over France, to eat with good crusty bread, some cheese, and a bottle of wine, by the side of the road somewhere. Practically every restaurant, no matter how humble, will have *charcuterie* in some form as a first course, and *pâté de campagne*, country loaf, is likely to be one of them. They vary from place to place, and season to season, and can be anything from a simple mixture of well-seasoned liver and pork, mounded and baked with bacon strips on top, to more complicated mixtures that include ground veal and are cooked in a water bath.

One thing that is apt to discourage an American cook from trying a typical French country pâté is what seems to be an inordinate amount of pork fat in the recipe, sometimes as much as, or more than, each of the other meats. Actually, much of it cooks away, and a lot more is removed before serving when it has solidified on the outside of the loaf. We have chosen recipes with less extra fat than some, but it is an essential ingredient to achieve the texture and taste of a real pâté de campagne.

For this pâté, veal is added to the basic pork and liver, but the loaf is cooked the simple way, uncovered, with bacon on top. It is what is called a "coarse" pâté, partly because some of the ingredients are in larger pieces than others, and partly to distinguish it from a smooth, spreadable pâté. It is served in slices, the dark pieces of liver and the little white specks of pork fat and bread contrasting attractively with the ground pork and veal. Served as a first course, on a lettuce leaf, with a little parsley or watercress, it would be accompanied in France by small sour gherkins, called *cornichons*, available in specialty food shops here, or by Ratatouille.* With good French or Italian bread and young fresh red wine like Beaujolais, Mâcon Rouge, or California Zinfandel, the pâté can precede practically anything: roast or chops, stew or casserole, fish or spaghetti.

As a main course for luncheon or supper, the pâté would be nice with hard-cooked eggs and mayonnaise, Grated Carrot Salad* and cucumbers in French Dressing* on lettuce, sour gherkins, and plenty of crusty bread and cheese. Fresh fruit or a fruit salad could top off this cool repast. Make the pâté one day and serve it the next, or up to a week later. It improves with keeping, well wrapped in foil and refrigerated.

For 8-cup loaf pan (9" x 5" x 3")

 1 pound ground pork shoulder
½ pound ground veal
¼ pound fresh pork fat (preferably from the loin,
    but fresh-ham fat will do)
½ pound pork or beef liver
¼ cup Cognac

2–3 slices firm white home-style bread, crusts removed
½ cup milk

 1 egg
2¼ teaspoons salt
½ teaspoon freshly ground black pepper
⅛ teaspoon mace
⅛ teaspoon allspice
½ teaspoon thyme
⅛ teaspoon rosemary, finely crumbled
 1 small bay leaf, finely crumbled
 2 cloves garlic, minced

    Bacon slices for top and bottom of loaf

 2 tablespoons chopped parsley
    Parsley sprigs or watercress to garnish

Put the ground pork and veal into a large mixing bowl. Dice the
pork fat into small cubes, ⅛ to ¼ inch. The fat sticks together
quite a bit but will separate when it is mixed with the other meats.
Pat the liver dry with paper towels, trim off any fat and membranes,
and cut into ¼-inch dice. Mix the fat and liver with the pork and
veal. Pour in the Cognac and mix again.

Crumble or carefully tear the bread into coarse crumbs, to make 1 cupful. Allow the crumbs to soak in the milk for a few minutes and then mix with the meats.

In a small bowl, beat the egg lightly and add all the seasonings and the garlic. Add to the contents of the large bowl and mix thoroughly, first with a wooden spoon; then, when the mixture dries somewhat, with the hands.

Put a layer of bacon strips on the bottom of an 8-cup loaf pan and pack in the loaf mixture, pressing into the corners and patting to avoid air holes. Mound the loaf slightly and cover with bacon slices.

Bake, uncovered, in a 350° oven for 1 to 1¼ hours or until loaf has shrunk from the sides of the pan and juices run clear, not pink or opaque, when loaf is pricked and pressed. Remove the loaf from the oven and allow it to cool in the pan. Do not pour off the juice; a lot of it is fat, but underneath is good meat extract. When the loaf is completely cool, cover and refrigerate overnight.

To unmold, run a knife around the edge of the loaf, hold the pan briefly in an inch or so of hot water, and slide the loaf out onto a platter or cutting board, right side up, to show the browned top. Trim the hardened fat from the sides, carefully preserving any jellied or liquid juices. Spoon juices over the loaf. Serve well sprinkled with chopped parsley and surrounded with lots of parsley sprigs or watercress, or serve already sliced. Makes about 16 half-inch slices.

Pâté de Campagne Coach House
Veal, Pork, and Chicken-Liver Loaf

Here is a country pâté from one of New York's most sophisticated restaurants, Leon Lianides' Coach House, in Greenwich Village. A marvelous mixture of veal, pork, and chicken livers, Cognac, spices, and dried mushrooms soaked in Sherry, it is worth the search for the large loaf pan needed to cook it in. I make it in a stainless steel loaf pan about 10 inches long, 5 inches wide, and 4 inches deep, which is a restaurant supply item. It holds 10 cups, or 2½ quarts; a pan of any smaller volume would not be big enough. A pan holding 12 cups, or 3 quarts, would also be good, but it must be deep and narrow, or the loaf will be too shallow, and the cooking time will be affected. If you have no meat grinder, buy the pork and veal already ground and then chop the pork fat and soaked mushrooms as finely as possible. Some butchers will grind the pork, veal, and pork fat together for you, so all you have to chop by hand is the mushrooms.

An unusual touch at the Coach House, which I had never encountered before, is Cumberland Sauce* offered with the pâté, a piquant sauce of Port, currant jelly, and citrus fruit. The merest spoonful sprinkled over has an interesting effect on the pâté. It is not, of course, necessary, but it is fun for the adventurous, and the sauce keeps, to be used with other things, such as ham, tongue, chicken, or turkey.

The pâté could be followed by something simple—a roast, chops, or pepper steak (Steak au Poivre) or something more elegant: roast duckling or a rack of lamb. The green salad could have tiny French black olives and a crumble of feta cheese on it and be followed by a cheese tray and/or some fine French pastry.

The pâté goes with red or white wine. The white could be a Chardonnay from Mâcon or California or a Muscadet from the Loire. The red could be a Pomerol or St. Émilion from Bordeaux.

The pâté improves with keeping and will stay good for ten days in the pan if it is covered with a layer of melted lard when it is chilled and then covered with foil when the lard hardens. To use just part of the loaf, turn it out as directed in the recipe and scrape off and reserve the lard from the portion you want to use. Spread the reserved lard over the exposed end of the rest, put it back in the pan, cover, and refrigerate until needed again.

For 10-cup loaf pan (10″ x 5″ x 4″) or terrine

1 pound boneless pork shoulder
1 pound boneless veal
¾ pound fresh pork fat (from the loin or from a fresh ham)
½ cup dried mushrooms
¼ cup Amontillado Sherry

1 pound chicken livers
6 cloves garlic, coarsely chopped
3 eggs
¼ cup heavy cream
½ cup Cognac

3 teaspoons salt
2 teaspoons white pepper
½ teaspoon allspice
½ teaspoon cinnamon

½ cup flour
⅓ cup pistachio nuts, coarsely chopped

¾–1 pound bacon

Parsley sprigs or watercress to garnish

Soak mushrooms in Sherry for a minimum of 20 minutes. Packaged dried mushrooms can be found in specialty food stores, but if you can find European bulk-sold ones, in Italian or bulk-spice stores, they are better. The good ones are expensive, but you need only ½ to ¾ ounce to make ½ cup.

Grind together the pork, veal, and pork fat with the mushrooms, adding any unabsorbed juices surrounding the mushrooms.

Pâté de Campagne Coach House / 33

Trim yellow fat from the chicken livers and purée them in an electric blender with the garlic, eggs, cream, and Cognac. Gradually add to the blender about a third of the ground meat mixture.

Blend in the seasonings and combine the blender contents with the rest of the meat mixture in a large mixing bowl. Mix well.

Sprinkle in the flour, mixing well, and stir in the pistachio nuts.

Line the bottom of a 10-cup loaf pan or terrine with bacon slices. Line the long sides with bacon (it adheres) and then the short sides, letting the ends hang over. Reserve some bacon to complete the covering of the top of the loaf.

Pour the mixture into the bacon-lined pan carefully, gently patting to avoid air holes. Cover tightly with a double thickness of foil. Place in a larger shallow pan filled with hot water to come halfway up the side of the loaf pan. Set in a preheated 400° oven for 3 hours. Replace hot water if it boils away. Remove the foil and continue baking until the top is slightly brown, 15 to 20 minutes. Remove from the oven; do not pour off juices. Place a clean piece of oiled foil lightly on the top and weight with a brick or a slightly smaller pan with some heavy objects in it (see Introduction). When loaf is completely cool, remove weight, cover well with the foil, and refrigerate for two days before serving.

To unmold, run a knife around the edges of the loaf, hold the pan briefly in an inch or so of hot water, and slide out onto a platter or board, right side up, to show the browned top. Serve surrounded by parsley or watercress, to be sliced at the table, or already cut into slices. Yields about 30 large quarter-inch slices.

Pâté de Campagne Pujol
Pork and Liver Loaf

One of several popular pâtés at the René Pujol French restaurant in New York, this pâté de campagne has a predominant liver taste, although there is twice as much pork as liver in it. It is slightly more delicate than the one that follows, since it has fresh pork fat to line the pan rather than salty fatback, but is very much like it in its seasonings. Sliceable and a little coarse in texture, it is hearty in its way and makes a fine first course, before roast, chops, stew, or casserole. Served as part of a buffet, it could be accompanied by crisp raw vegetables with Green Sauce,* a platter of deviled eggs well sprigged with parsley, Salade Niçoise au Riz,* a tray of good cheeses, and plenty of crusty bread. The wine could be fresh and young and red—a Beaujolais, Mâcon Rouge, or California Zinfandel.

Make the pâté one day, serve it the next. It improves with keeping, well wrapped and refrigerated.

For 8-cup loaf pan (9" x 5" x 3")

1 pound pork or beef liver, trimmed of membranes
1 medium onion
2 cloves garlic

2 pounds ground pork shoulder
1 medium bay leaf, finely crumbled
½ teaspoon thyme
½ teaspoon freshly ground black pepper
1 tablespoon salt
¼ cup Cognac

   Thin sheets of pork loin fat for top and bottom of loaf

2 tablespoons chopped parsley
   Watercress or parsley sprigs as garnish

Put the liver, onion, and garlic through the meat grinder or food mill or chop very fine. It will all be quite liquid, particularly if the grinder or food mill is used, but do not drain. In a large bowl, mix thoroughly with the pork, spices, and Cognac, first with a wooden spoon or rubber spatula and then with the hands. The mixture will be moist, but it dries out a bit with mixing.

Line the bottom of an 8-cup loaf pan with fat pork sheets and pack in the meat mixture, pushing into the corners and patting to make sure there are no air holes. Cover with sheets of fat and seal the pan with foil. Set the pan in a preheated 300° oven and cook for 1¼ to 1½ hours, or until no pinkish juices are coming out and a metal skewer comes out clean after being plunged into the loaf. Remove from the oven, loosen the foil around the edges, and place a brick, or some canned goods in a smaller loaf pan, on top of the loaf. This presses out fat and makes the loaf firmer for slicing. Do not pour off juices. When completely cool, refrigerate overnight, with the weight still on.

To unmold, run a knife around the edge, stand the pan in an inch or so of hot water for a few moments, and invert onto a platter, giving a short jerk to dislodge the loaf. Carefully remove and discard the solidified fat from the edges, but preserve any clear, slightly jellied juices which cling to it and spoon them over the loaf. Wipe the edge of the platter clean, sprinkle the loaf with chopped parsley, and surround with parsley sprigs or watercress. Or, if you dislike the look of the pork fat on what is now the top of the loaf, serve it already cut into ⅜-inch slices. Makes about 20 slices.

Pâté de Foie de Porc
Pork Liver Pâté

Although it is mainly liver, this pâté has a pâté de campagne taste because of the heartiness of salt pork in it, and the fatback that lines the loaf pan. It cannot be spread like the Pâté de Foies de Volaille that follows it. It is firm and sliceable and fine picnic fare, as well as making a typically French first course, served on lettuce with *cornichons* or sour gherkins, and toast or crusty bread. With the versatility of the other pâtés de campagne, it can be followed by the same variety of main courses. In a buffet that included cold shrimp with Green Sauce* or a poached fish with mayonnaise, the wine could be a white like a Riesling from the Rhine or the Moselle, or an Anjou or Grenache Rosé.

Make the pâté one day, serve it the next or up to a week later. It improves with keeping, well wrapped in foil and refrigerated.

For 5-cup loaf pan (8½″ x 4½″ x 2½″)

1½ pounds pork liver (or beef liver)
½ pound lean pork
½ pound salt pork
1 small onion
2 teaspoons flour

1 large egg
½ teaspoon salt
¼ teaspoon freshly ground black pepper
¼ teaspoon thyme
1 small bay leaf, finely crumbled
1 tablespoon finely chopped fresh parsley
2 tablespoons Cognac

¾–1 pound thin slices of fatback *or* fat salt pork with no streaks of lean

2 tablespoons chopped parsley
Watercress or parsley sprigs to garnish

Trim fat and membranes from the liver, pat dry, and grind with the pork, salt pork, and onion. If you have no meat grinder, chop them all very fine together. Place the mixture in a large mixing bowl and sprinkle with the flour. Work the flour in with a wooden spoon or pestle.

In a small bowl, beat the egg and add the seasonings, parsley, and Cognac. Add, a little at a time, to the meat mixture, blending well after each addition.

Rinse the fatback or salt pork slices in cold water if there is obvious salt on the surface, pat dry, and line a 5-cup loaf pan with it, saving some for the top of the loaf. Whether you get the butcher to slice the fat for you or do it yourself, chances are the pieces won't fit the pan perfectly. You can either fit them in like a jigsaw puzzle or pound them between two sheets of waxed paper to make them thinner and weld them in larger sheets, out of which can be cut pieces that just fit each surface. (Use the pan itself as the pattern.)

Pack the meat mixture into the pan, being careful to avoid air holes. Mound the loaf slightly in the center, and cover with the sliced fatback. Place the pan in a larger, shallow pan filled with hot water to come halfway up the side of the loaf pan and place, uncovered, in a preheated 375° oven. Bake for 1¼ hours, or until the juices run clear, not pink and cloudy, when the loaf is pricked and pressed. Remove from the oven, cool to room temperature, and refrigerate.

To unmold, remove fat from the top, run a knife around the edge, immerse the pan briefly in an inch or so of hot water, and slide out, browned side up, onto waxed paper for trimming. Remove solidified, lardlike fat, and the sliced fat around the loaf, carefully preserving the jellied juices that adhere. Put the loaf on a platter or bread board and spread the meat juices on top. If it is to be presented whole and carved at the table, sprinkle finely chopped parsley over it and surround with parsley sprigs or watercress; otherwise serve in ⅜-inch slices, garnished in the same way. Makes about sixteen slices.

Pâté de Foies de Volaille
Chicken Liver Pâté

This is the smooth, rich spread that many people think of when the word "pâté" is mentioned. The most famous and expensive version is, of course, Foie Gras, the whole fat liver of a force-fed goose, often cooked in Madeira and Cognac, and called Foie Gras Truffé when studded with truffles. Then there are the mixtures of best and lesser-quality foie gras called Bloc de Foie Gras and Bloc de Foie Gras Truffé when it contains truffles. Finally, there are the mixtures containing a certain proportion of foie gras, called, in order of decreasing amounts of real foie gras, Purée de Foie Gras, Purée de Foie d'Oie, and Mousse de Foie Gras. These are all available in cans, and none of them are inexpensive. Cans labeled Pâté de Foie Gras can be anything, not being covered by French law as to the proportion of best quality fat goose liver they contain.

A splendid alternative is this pâté of chicken livers, with butter and cream supplying the fat and Cognac, Madeira, lemon, herbs, and spices the flavor. It is easy to make in the blender. Unlike most pâtés and terrines, it can be used the day it is made if it is done early enough to allow for a couple of hours of chilling. It is particularly good on thin dry toast but is also good on French or Italian bread. Served as a little first course, or as a buffet item, it could be presented in its container on a platter or in a shallow basket, surrounded by toast and sliced crusty bread, with a spreader, for people to help themselves. No butter is required.

A versatile pâté, it goes very well with both cocktails and red or white wine and is elegant enough to be superb with Champagne.

For 1-cup jar or pot

- ½ pound chicken livers
- 2 tablespoons butter
- ⅛ teaspoon salt
- ⅛ teaspoon freshly ground black pepper
- 2 tablespoons Cognac

- ½ clove garlic (the size of a pea), cut up
- 2 tablespoons soft butter
- 1 tablespoon heavy cream (more if needed)
  Pinch of Quatre-Épices* or allspice
  Pinch each of thyme and basil
- 1 teaspoon lemon juice
- ¼ teaspoon Madeira
  Salt and pepper to taste

1–2 tablespoons melted butter for the top

Pat the livers dry and trim off any yellow fat or membrane that clings to them; also any black or greenish spots. Cut them into uniformly sized pieces, about 1 inch square. Heat the butter in a small skillet until the foam has almost subsided, and put in the livers. Cook for 3 or 4 minutes, or until the livers have turned light brown but are still pink inside. Sprinkle with salt and pepper, and remove livers from the pan to a plate or small bowl. Turn off heat. Pour the Cognac into the pan and stir to mix with the pan juices and to incorporate bits on the bottom. Pour this liquid into the blender.

Add all the rest of the ingredients to the blender, except the additional salt and pepper and the melted butter for the top. Cover and start blender; then add the livers, a few at a time. Add any juice that has come out of the cooked livers while they waited. Blend until just smooth, stopping to scrape down the sides occasionally. Add a little more cream if the mixture gets too dry. It should be a soft pudding texture; it firms up when cold. Remove to a small bowl and add salt and pepper to taste.

Pour into a 1-cup jar or pot, smooth the surface, and cover with a layer of melted butter to keep it from drying out. Refrigerate for 2 hours. Serve from the pot, with thin dry toast.

Chopped Chicken Livers, Jewish Style

Smooth and unctuous though the preceding Pâté de Foies de Volaille is, many people prefer the texture and hearty taste of this next version. On the theory that it's-nice-to-have-both, this recipe is offered. The result can be a surprise and delight to those who have never encountered chopped chicken livers with the magic addition of grebenes, the crisp tidbits (cracklings) that are produced by the slow rendering of chicken fat with onions. The slightly coarse spread makes a fine hors-d'oeuvre to have with drinks, on rye or pumpernickel bread, or a first course on French bread, with a hearty red wine such as Côte Rôtie or Hermitage from the Rhône, or a full white like a Vouvray or a California Sauvignon Blanc. It can also be part of a buffet, along with one of the other cold loaves in the book and the things suggested to go with it. Good for a picnic too.

The recipe came to me from Rome, of all places. It and a supply of grebenes and chicken fat were hand-carried to me from Babs Bloom by a mutual friend, and I hope you agree that no book of pâtés should be without it.

This can be served the day it is made, allowing time for chilling. It keeps for about three days, well covered and refrigerated.

For 1½-cup jar or pot

  1 pound chicken fat (can include some skin), finely chopped
  1 medium onion, finely chopped

  1 small onion, finely chopped
  ½ pound chicken livers

  1 hard-cooked egg
  1 small onion, minced
     Salt and pepper

In a heavy skillet, over a low flame, slowly cook the chicken fat, pouring off the liquid fat into a clean receptacle as it is rendered. When the pieces of fat have lost their bright yellow color, add the chopped medium onion and continue the slow cooking, stirring and pouring off the liquid for later use, until the bits in the pan are crisp and brown. Drain and reserve. These crisp particles are grebenes, and some will be added to the chopped livers later for added texture and taste. This recipe makes about 1¾ cups of fat and about ¾ cup of grebenes. Both can be kept almost indefinitely in jars in the refrigerator. Grebenes can be recrisped briefly in a hot pan before using after refrigeration.

Wipe the pan and put in 1 tablespoon of the rendered fat. Pat the livers dry and trim off any yellow fat and membranes and any black or greenish spots. Heat the fat in the pan and put the livers in, with the small chopped onion, and cook until there is no more liquid in the pan and no pink comes out of the livers when they are pricked. Use a little more fat if needed.

Chop the livers with half the hard-cooked egg and the small minced onion. Add salt and pepper to taste, and enough of the reserved chicken fat to make the desired texture—about 2 tablespoons. The mixture should be spreadable but not pastelike, as it would be if done in a blender or grinder. Mix in a tablespoon or more of grebenes and make into a mound. Finely chop the rest of the egg white and sprinkle over, and sieve the rest of the egg yolk onto the top.

If you are preparing the dish for later use, reserve the half egg; put the finished mixture of liver and grebenes into a bowl or jar, smooth and flatten the top, and seal with a thin layer of melted chicken fat. Then, to serve after refrigeration, stir in the fat on the top, turn out, and form into a mound (or serve from the container) topped with the chopped egg white and sieved yolk, and serve with dry crisp toast. It makes about 1½ cups.

A favorite item in a Danish *kolde bord*, the cold table, this sliceable and spreadable liver loaf can be a fine addition to anyone's repertoire of cold loaves. Too rich for a main course, it nevertheless has many uses as part of a meal. Served on black bread as an open-faced sandwich, with Sweet-Sour Cucumbers,* it is customarily accompanied by tiny glasses of aquavit, but a smaller version could go with cocktails; sliced on a plate with French bread, and accompanied by a hearty red wine, it could serve as a first course. For a splendid picnic, it could go with cold chicken, hard-cooked eggs, crisp raw vegetables, and pickles. Dark bread or a crusty loaf, plenty of cheese and fruit, and beer or red wine would round out the feast.

For a cold buffet, somewhat Danish style, a number of good things could share the table with Leverpostej. A few suggestions: potato salad, pickled beets, deviled eggs, cold shrimp, smoked salmon, raw mushroom salad, cucumbers in Sour Cream with Dill,* pickled herring, sweet and sour red cabbage, sliced tomatoes with anchovies, salami or other good cold cuts, a bowl of lettuce and watercress, thinly sliced onions, a tray of cheeses (one of them Danish blue), mayonnaise, pickles and mustard, and a great basket of assorted breads—pumpernickel, rye, and Italian—as well as some thin Scandinavian crackers.

After an icy aquavit or chilled Amontillado Sherry, beer would go well with the buffet. If Leverpostej is served as a first course before a hearty meat course, the wine could be red, a Beaujolais or California Zinfandel. If seafood or fish were to follow, a white would be better—a Graves or a Rhine.

Make Leverpostej one day, serve it the next, or up to five days later. It improves with keeping, well wrapped and refrigerated.

For 5-cup loaf pan (8½″ x 4½″ x 2½″)

    1 pound fresh pork liver (or beef liver)
    ½ pound fresh pork fat (from the loin, or from a fresh ham) in 1-inch pieces
    1 small onion, coarsely chopped (about ½ cup)
    3 flat anchovy fillets, drained

    2 tablespoons butter
    2 tablespoons flour
    ½ cup milk
    ½ cup heavy cream

    2 eggs
    1¼ teaspoons salt
    1¼ teaspoons Quatre-Épices* *or* ¾ teaspoon white pepper and ⅛ teaspoon each ground cloves, ground ginger, and ground nutmeg

    ½ pound bacon slices to line bottom and sides of the pan

Trim membranes from the liver and cut into 1-inch pieces. Combine liver, pork fat, onion, and anchovies in a large mixing bowl.

In a small saucepan, melt the butter and stir in the flour. Remove from the heat and whisk in the milk and cream. Put back on the heat and bring to a boil, stirring constantly. Simmer for a few minutes, still stirring, until sauce is smooth and very thick. Cool.

Divide the meat mixture into three parts and mix in the blender a third at a time, moistening each with a third of the cream sauce. Remove each batch when smooth to a large bowl.

Lightly beat the eggs and add the salt and seasonings. Mix thoroughly with the liver mixture. (The result will be very liquid.)

Line a 5-cup loaf pan or mold with bacon. Cover the bottom first and then press slices on the sides and ends, cutting pieces to fit when necessary. (The bacon will adhere to the pan.) Pour in the liver mixture. Do not put bacon on the top; it will sink in. Cover with heavy foil, sealing the edges well. Place in a larger shallow pan and pour in boiling water to come halfway up the sides of the loaf pan. Set in a preheated 350° oven and cook for 1¾ hours. Remove from the oven and allow to cool with the foil loosened. When loaf has come to room temperature, cover and refrigerate overnight.

To unmold, run a knife around the edge of the loaf, immerse the pan in an inch or so of hot water for a moment or two, and slide out onto a platter or cutting board, right side up. Yields about 15 half-inch slices.

Rillettes
Potted Pork

Rillettes are a specialty of the Loire Valley in France. They are shreds of pork with fat, packed in little pots, to be spread on bread or toast as an accompaniment for the wines of the district—cool glasses of Anjou rosé, red Chinon, or, particularly, white wines like Vouvray or Sancerre. It's a delicious way to start a meal and good to have along on a picnic.

Rillettes come from the days when every part of the pig was utilized. The pork and its fat would keep for weeks, even months, sealed with a layer of lard and stored in a cool place. Fresh sowbelly, the cut now used for bacon, was most often used for the making. Today sowbelly can be difficult to find, so this recipe calls for lean pork shoulder and an equal amount of fat salt pork. Even with the excess salt washed off, the salt pork is salty, so it is unlikely that you will need to add any more salt. If you would like to have more control of saltiness, simmer the salt pork for 10 minutes in plenty of water to remove much of the salt, and then use salt to taste when the rillettes are cooked.

The following recipe makes about 3 cups, which will fill four 6-ounce pots, jars, or custard cups, and will keep for four weeks in the refrigerator, covered just with its own fat and a piece of foil or plastic. We have not personally tried any longer storage, but we might venture six weeks if the pots were sterilized first.

Rillettes can be used the day they are made, with time allowed for chilling, but they are better the following day, or up to four weeks later. In attractive pots or jars, they make a fine hostess present, or that little gift of something good to eat to give at Christmas.

For four 6-ounce jars, pots, or custard cups

1 pound lean pork shoulder, in 2-inch pieces or squares
1 pound fat salt pork, with little or no lean, in 2-inch pieces or squares
    Water to cover
½ teaspoon pepper
½ teaspoon thyme
1 bay leaf

    Salt to taste, if needed

Put the pieces of pork shoulder in a heavy, lidded, flameproof casserole, preferably enameled ironware. Rinse the salt pork under cold running water to remove the salt from the surface, and add to the pork shoulder. Add cold water to cover. Bring to a boil, add pepper, thyme, and bay leaf, cover, and place in preheated 250° oven. Cook for 4 hours, checking occasionally to be sure that only the merest simmer is being maintained and that the pork is not drying out. If it does seem to be drying, add a little boiling water. At the end of the 4 hours, the pork should be very soft and the fat almost completely liquid. Remove from the oven and allow to cool slightly.

Discard the bay leaf and strain, reserving the drained-off fat. Put ¼ cup of the melted fat into the blender, then add a quarter of the pork, whirling briefly to break it up but not long enough to make a mush. Remove to a bowl and repeat until all the pork is used. Mix all the batches together, using two forks, to make sure the pork is evenly shredded. Add melted fat to make the mixture soft.

The rillettes should have a slightly salty taste, and the salt pork will probably have supplied enough salt. If not, add salt to taste. Put the mixture into the pots, jars, or custard cups, leaving about ½ inch of room on top, and pour melted fat over to fill the containers. When thoroughly cool, refrigerate and cover with foil or plastic pressed on to the fat when it has hardened. To serve, remove the solid fat from the top (but preserve it to cover leftovers) and set out the container with a small spreading knife and a basket of good bread and some thin dry toast.

Pâté Chez Nous
Beef, Pork, and Veal Loaf in Aspic

The supermarket mixture of beef, pork, and veal is used for this loaf, our original Pâté of the House. Varied with a change of seasonings or by the addition of nuts, pimientos, or olives; refined by the omission of beef and the addition of spices; evolved into terrines and *pâtés en croûte*, it is one of the things we often like to make and feel a need to have around, for an hors-d'oeuvre, first course, luncheon, buffet, or bring-a-dish party.

For all its simplicity, this particular loaf has plenty of taste. Served as a first course, with *cornichons* (little sour gherkins), it could be followed by practically anything—roast, chops, steak, stew, or spaghetti—and a good, young, hearty red wine, such as a Mâcon or Beaujolais or a California Petite Sirah or Zinfandel, would go well with both courses. As a main course for luncheon or supper, the loaf would be fine with cold Ratatouille,* a leafy salad, crusty bread, cheese, and fruit; or with macaroni and cheese, Grated Carrot Salad* on lettuce, and Roquefort cheese and apples for dessert. For a buffet, the loaf might share the honors with a Quiche Lorraine and a bowl of cold shrimp with a Green Sauce* dip. Endive or celery and green pepper in strips, with radishes for something crisp, and a salad of cooked green beans or asparagus in Vinaigrette Dressing* or Celery Root Rémoulade,* a cheese tray, and a basket of assorted breads could complete the array. A good rosé wine such as a Tavel, an Anjou, or a Grenache from California would go with everything, or, for those who like to enjoy a buffet in courses, a white wine such as a Muscadet or California Chardonnay could be served with the *quiche* and shrimp, and one of the suggested reds for the pâté and cheese.

Make this pâté one day, serve it the next. It is still better served two to six days after cooking. Well wrapped and refrigerated, it will keep up to a week.

For 8-cup loaf pan (9" x 5" x 3")

2 pounds ground meat, equal parts beef, veal, pork
1 large celery stalk, chopped
⅓ cup uncooked oatmeal
¼ cup finely chopped fresh parsley

1 egg
2 cloves garlic, chopped
2 teaspoons salt
½ teaspoon freshly ground black pepper
¾ teaspoon oregano
¼ teaspoon thyme
⅓ cup dry red wine

2 small bay leaves
Bacon slices to cover

1 envelope unflavored gelatin (1½ envelopes for a picnic or in hot weather)
2 tablespoons Cognac
1½ cups canned beef broth (a 13¾-ounce can ready-to-use, cooked down to 1½ cups)

2 tablespoons chopped parsley
Parsley sprigs or watercress to garnish

Put the ground meats, celery, oatmeal, and parsley in a large mixing bowl.

In a small mixing bowl, lightly beat the egg. Using a strong fork, mash the garlic with the salt on a saucer until there are no large chunks. Add, with the pepper, oregano, and thyme, to the egg. Add the wine and combine with the meat mixture in the large mixing bowl. Mix well. If it is very dry, add a little more wine.

Pack the mixture into a buttered 8-cup loaf pan, pressing into corners and patting to avoid air holes. Flatten the top and push a bay leaf down between loaf and pan at the center of the long sides. Cover loaf with bacon slices.

Place, uncovered, in a preheated 350° oven for 1 to 1¼ hours, until loaf has shrunk a bit from the sides and juices run clear, not pink or opaque, when loaf is pricked and pressed. Remove from the oven and allow to stand for 15 minutes. With two spatulas or flat egg-lifters, carefully move the loaf from side to side and end to end of the pan to detach it from the bottom. Do not pour off juices.

In a 2-cup measuring cup, moisten the gelatin with the Cognac. Bring the broth to a boil and add to the gelatin, stirring until it is dissolved. Pour this mixture (aspic) over the loaf, moving the loaf as you pour until it is floating in the middle of the aspic. Set a saucer or cup on the loaf to keep it down if it has a tendency to float above the liquid. (Both loaf and aspic should still be hot for this process, so the fat will be floated to the top and will appear hardened at the bottom of the loaf when it is chilled and inverted for serving later.) Cool to room temperature, cover, and refrigerate for 8 hours or overnight.

To unmold, run a knife around the edge of the loaf, immerse the pan briefly in a basin of hot water, and turn out upside down onto a cold platter. Remove bay leaves. Wipe the edge of the platter clean, sprinkle the loaf with plenty of chopped parsley, and surround with parsley or watercress. Yields about 25 quarter-inch slices.

Pâté Maison #1
Veal and Pork Loaf in Aspic

Another pâté of the house, this is one that evolved from the original Pâté Chez Nous (preceding recipe). It has the refinement of using veal and pork alone, without beef, and the seasonings are more complicated. It has nuts and black olives in it and, like all our house pâtés and their variations, is coated in aspic.

Served as a first course, this pâté or either of the variations which follow can be offered on small plates with some of their garnish, with or without lettuce. Either white or red wine goes with them, and crusty bread is essential. They can be followed by a simple roast, chops, steak, or a braised meat dish, with vegetables, salad, and a cheese course. Fresh fruit, or a compote with a touch of liqueur, and coffee would round out a most satisfactory dinner.

As main-course dishes, since they have no sauce or gravy, these pâtés need a good self-sufficient starchy accompaniment, such as Potatoes in Cream Sauce,* Pommes Anna,* buttered noodles, or a creamy macaroni. Supplemented with a first course of hard-cooked eggs with mayonnaise, or smoked salmon, and with a cheese course between the salad and dessert, they would even make a more formal meal.

For a lighter luncheon or supper, these pâtés are fine with just a salad and simple dessert, or they could go with a cheese or spinach soufflé, accompanied by a moist vegetable such as asparagus or sautéed sliced tomatoes. Good wine and good bread would make this simple meal a feast. Dessert could be just coffee and liqueur.

Another way to serve these pâtés is for a buffet, using a good substantial soup such as black bean or pea soup in a handsome tureen as a first course and with the pâté, cold shrimp, cheeses, and deviled eggs to follow. With this, instead of salad, a great bowl of crisp things like radishes, raw cauliflower, celery, green pepper strips, and watercress to dip in Green Sauce* would be perfect. A rich, extravagant dessert wouldn't be too much afterward; let yourself go.

Wines to go with this group of pâtés can be white or red. Whites could be a white Burgundy, like a Meursault, or a Vouvray from the Loire; reds could be a red Burgundy, like a Volnay or Monthélie, or a Côtes du Rhône.

Make these pâtés one day, serve them the next. They are still better two to six days after cooking. Keep them well covered with foil and refrigerated until used.

For 8-cup loaf pan (9" x 5" x 3")

- 1¼ pounds ground veal
- 1¼ pounds ground pork shoulder
- ½ cup uncooked oatmeal
- ¼ cup finely chopped fresh parsley
- 2 celery stalks, chopped
- ¼ cup (2 ounces) pistachio nuts, shelled and peeled, *or* ¼ cup pine nuts
- ⅓ cup Cognac

- 1 medium onion, finely chopped
- ½ cup Amontillado Sherry

- 1 egg
- 2½ teaspoons salt
- 2 cloves garlic, chopped
- ¼ teaspoon freshly ground black pepper
- ½ teaspoon marjoram
- ½ teaspoon thyme
- ⅛ teaspoon rosemary, crumbled
- 1 teaspoon Quatre-Épices* *or* ½ teaspoon white pepper and ⅛ teaspoon each ground ginger, ground nutmeg, ground cloves

- 10–12 pitted black olives
- 2 bay leaves
  Bacon slices to cover

- 1 envelope unflavored gelatin (1½ envelopes for a picnic or in hot weather)
- 2 tablespoons Cognac or Amontillado Sherry
- 1½ cups stock *or* a 13¾-ounce can ready-to-use beef broth cooked down to 1½ cups

1 tablespoon chopped pimientos
2 tablespoons chopped parsley
   Parsley sprigs or watercress

Put the veal, pork, oatmeal, parsley, celery, and nuts in a large mixing bowl. Pour in the Cognac.

In a small saucepan, slowly cook the onion with the Sherry until the Sherry is reduced by half. Add to the meats and mix lightly. Allow to stand for an hour.

In a small bowl, lightly beat the egg. Using a strong fork, mash the garlic with the salt on a saucer until there are no large chunks, and add with the seasonings to the egg. Add to the contents of the large bowl and mix well.

Butter an 8-cup loaf pan and pack in the meat mixture, pressing into corners and patting to avoid air holes. Press the olives into the loaf in a long row down the center and fill in the holes above them. Flatten the top and push a bay leaf down between loaf and pan at the center of the long sides. Cover the loaf with bacon slices, and bake, uncovered, in a preheated 350° oven, for 1¼ to 1½ hours, or until loaf has shrunk from the sides and juices run clear, not pink or opaque, when loaf is pricked and pressed. Remove loaf from the oven and allow it to cool for about 15 minutes. With a spatula, gently move the loaf from side to side and end to end in the pan to free it from the bottom. Do not pour off juices.

In a 2-cup measure, moisten gelatin with the Cognac or Sherry. Heat the broth just to boiling point and add to the gelatin, stirring to dissolve. Pour this aspic slowly over the loaf while both aspic and loaf are still hot. Pour in as much as the pan will take; leftover aspic can be saved for other uses or cooled, chilled, and served chopped around the loaf. The aspic permeates the loaf, filling every crevice and displacing the fat, which floats to the top. (When the loaf is chilled and turned out of the pan, the fat appears as a neat solid layer on the bottom and can easily be avoided by calorie counters.)

Cool the loaf and chill overnight. To unmold, run a knife around the edges and set the pan in a few inches of hot water for a second or two. Hold a platter over the pan and reverse, giving a slight jerk to dislodge the loaf. Remove bay leaves. Wipe the platter clean around the loaf and sprinkle the top with pimiento and chopped parsley; surround with parsley sprigs or watercress. This loaf yields about 15 half-inch slices and can also be sliced more thinly.

To make a loaf which is more delicate in taste, follow the foregoing recipe, changing the last five seasoning ingredients to

1 teaspoon freshly ground black pepper
1 teaspoon basil
¼ teaspoon thyme
⅛ teaspoon allspice

Second Variation

Substituting chicken livers for part of the veal and adding juniper berries make an interesting change in the loaf and provide an attractive pattern in the slices. Follow the original Pâté Maison #1 recipe, using these ingredients:

    1 pound ground veal
    ¼ pound chicken livers, cut in ¼–½-inch pieces
    1¼ pounds ground pork shoulder
    ½ cup uncooked oatmeal
    ¼ cup finely chopped fresh parsley
    2 celery stalks, chopped
    ⅓ cup Cognac

    1 medium onion, finely chopped
    ½ cup Amontillado Sherry

    1 egg
    2 cloves garlic, chopped
 2½ teaspoons salt
    ½ teaspoon freshly ground black pepper
    8 juniper berries, crushed
    1 teaspoon Bell's poultry seasoning
    2 bay leaves
      Bacon slices to cover

    1 envelope unflavored gelatin (1½ for a picnic or in hot weather)
    2 tablespoons Cognac or Amontillado Sherry
 1½ cups stock *or* a 13¾-ounce can ready-to-use beef broth cooked
      down to 1½ cups

    1 tablespoon chopped pimientos
    2 tablespoons chopped parsley
      Parsley sprigs or watercress

Pâté Maison #2
Veal and Bacon Loaf

This pâté, with its hint of spices, is made with ground veal; chopped bacon supplies flavor and the necessary fat. Unlike the other house pâtés, it has no cereal filler—just a sprinkle of flour. Chopped walnuts and grated lemon rind give it texture and freshness, and the consommé Madrilène used for its aspic gives it a handsome reddish-brown exterior. Since it contains no garlic, it is perhaps less strong than the others. It would be particularly good preceding a main course of chicken, fish, or seafood, served with a little Celery Root Rémoulade,* but it can also be used in the ways suggested for Pâté Maison #1, with the same wide choice of wines.

Make this pâté one day, serve it the next. It is even better two to six days after cooking. Keep it well wrapped and refrigerated until used.

For 8-cup loaf pan (9″ x 5″ x 3″)

2½ pounds ground veal
  4 slices bacon, diced
  ½ cup chopped walnuts, in roughly ¼-inch pieces
  ¼ cup finely chopped fresh parsley
    Grated rind of 1 lemon
  ⅓ cup Cognac

  1 small onion, finely chopped (about ½ cup)
  1 tablespoon butter

  1 egg, lightly beaten
  ⅓ cup heavy cream
2¼ teaspoons salt
  ¾ teaspoon freshly ground black pepper
  ¼ teaspoon dried ginger
  ¼ teaspoon nutmeg
  ½ teaspoon thyme
  1 small bay leaf, crumbled
  2 tablespoons flour
    Bacon slices to cover

  1 envelope unflavored gelatin (1½ envelopes for a picnic or in
    hot weather)
  2 tablespoons Amontillado Sherry or Madeira
  1 thirteen-ounce can consommé Madrilène

  1 hard-cooked egg, sliced
  2 tablespoons finely chopped fresh parsley
    Parsley sprigs or watercress

Put the veal, diced bacon, nuts, parsley, and lemon rind in a large mixing bowl. Pour in the Cognac.

In a small saucepan, slowly cook the onion in the butter until it is limp but not brown. Add to the mixture in the bowl and mix lightly. Allow to stand for an hour.

In a smaller bowl, mix the beaten egg and cream together. Add the seasonings and beat into the meat mixture with a wooden spoon until everything is well mixed. Sprinkle in the flour, a little at a time, mixing after each addition.

Butter an 8-cup loaf pan and put in the mixture, patting and pressing to avoid air holes. Flatten the top and cover with bacon slices. Bake, uncovered, in a preheated 350° oven for 1¼ to 1½ hours, or until the loaf has shrunk from the sides and the juices run clear, not pink or opaque, when the loaf is pricked and pressed. Remove from the oven and allow to stand for 15 minutes. Do not pour off juices. With a spatula, gently move the loaf from side to side and end to end of the pan to free it from the bottom.

In a 2-cup measuring cup, moisten the gelatin with the Sherry or Madeira. Heat the consommé to the boiling point and add to the gelatin, stirring to dissolve completely. Pour slowly over the loaf while both the loaf and the aspic are still hot, until the pan is full. The pan should take all the aspic, but any left over can be cooled, chilled, and chopped to be served with the loaf. Cool the loaf and chill overnight in the refrigerator.

To unmold, run a knife around the edges and set the pan in a few inches of hot water for a moment or two. Hold a cold platter over the pan and reverse, giving a slight jerk to dislodge. Wipe the platter clean around the loaf and garnish the top of the loaf with overlapping egg slices. Sprinkle with parsley and surround with parsley sprigs or watercress. Yields about 25 quarter-inch slices.

TERRINES

It is hard to tell the difference between a pâté and a terrine; the names seem to be interchangeable. Actually, a terrine is the deep, straight-sided, oval or rectangular ovenware dish some pâtés are cooked in and served from, although it is much easier to serve them turned out on a platter or cutting board. In French restaurants, the terrine on the menu will be more expensive than the pâté and will generally be more elegant, containing less of the fresh pork fat that dominates many pâtés.

Terrine de Body
Veal and Bacon Terrine

Body, pronounced *bo-dee*, is the word for a young calf in the old Loire Valley province of Berry. This marvelous terrine lives up to two of the characteristics we have attributed to terrines in general; it is indeed rather expensive, and it certainly has elegance. The pan is not actually lined with bacon, but bacon is in alternate layers with the veal. Ideally, the bacon should be paper thin and the veal pounded until it is lacy, to make many layers. The terrine is still good, though, with packaged thinly sliced bacon and the veal as thin as you can pound it. Because of the layers, it doesn't slice as thinly, when cooked, as the ground meat loaves, but even so it yields about 15 half-inch slices.

Served as a first course, the terrine could be followed by a very special chicken dish, such as Poulet à la Crème or Suprème de Volaille. If you like the idea of following through with the veal taste, a creamy Blanquette de Veau or a Braised Roast of Veal would be excellent, and the same white wine, a Pouilly-Fuissé, Sancerre, or even Champagne, could go with both courses. Rice and a green vegetable could accompany the main course, with a leafy salad after. Following a cheese course of Brie or Camembert, dessert could be fresh fruit or a fruit salad.

As a main-course luncheon or supper dish, the terrine could be served with hard-cooked eggs with mayonnaise, a green salad, crusty bread, and cheese and fruit. In this case, the wine could be a simple young red, like a Beaujolais-Villages, or a great Burgundy or Bordeaux if the pocketbook will permit.

The terrine is made one day and served the next, or up to four or five days later. Keep it well wrapped and refrigerated. The flavor improves with keeping.

For 8-cup loaf pan (9" x 5" x 3")

  2 pounds veal scallops, pounded as thin as possible
1½ pounds thinly sliced bacon

  2 medium onions, finely chopped
¾ cup finely chopped fresh parsley
  1 teaspoon thyme
  1 teaspoon freshly ground black pepper
  1 bay leaf, finely crumbled
    Pinch of nutmeg

½ teaspoon unflavored gelatin for each layer
   Salt, if needed
½ cup dry white wine, *or* Amontillado Sherry, *or* Cognac

2 tablespoons chopped parsley
   Parsley sprigs or watercress to garnish

Figure out how much of the veal you will need for one layer, without overlapping, in an 8-cup loaf pan. Divide the rest of the veal into as many portions of the same amount as it will make. Divide the bacon into enough portions for one more layer than the veal.

Mix together the onions, parsley, thyme, pepper, bay leaf, and nutmeg. Divide the mixture into as many portions as you have of veal.

Put a layer of bacon in the bottom of the pan, cover with a layer of veal, and sprinkle with a portion of the onion-parsley-seasoning mixture, and the ½ teaspoon of unflavored gelatin. With good strong bacon, the terrine should not need any salt, but a lot of packaged bacon is very bland. If you have to use a bland bacon, sprinkle each layer with a little salt. Repeat the layers, not forgetting the gelatin on each, until everything is used, ending with bacon on the top. Pour in the wine, Sherry, or Cognac and allow to stand for a half hour, or several hours refrigerated.

Cover the pan well with heavy foil, and put a weight on top—a brick or the equivalent (see Introduction). Place the pan in a larger pan, with hot water to come halfway up the side of the loaf pan. Cook in a preheated 325° oven for 2 hours. Remove from the oven, loosen foil, but leave the brick in place. Do not pour off juices. When the loaf has come to room temperature, refrigerate, with the weight still on, until chilled and set, preferably overnight. The weight presses out the fat and keeps the layers flat for easier carving.

To unmold, set the pan briefly in hot water, run a knife around the edges, and invert onto a cold platter. Serve surrounded by watercress or parsley sprigs and with a sprinkling of chopped parsley on top. Or serve already cut. Yields about 15 half-inch slices.

First Variation

Use regular bacon for the bottom and the top of the loaf and thinly sliced Canadian bacon for the layers in between, alternating with the veal. If the butcher won't slice it thinly for you, buy it in a piece (about 1½ pounds) and slice it yourself. All the other ingredients remain the same. If the bacon is very bland, as it usually is, sprinkle each layer with a little salt.

Second Variation

Substitute pork or beef liver for the veal in the original recipe. The liver should be thinly sliced, which is easier to do if you slightly freeze the pieces before slicing. Unless you are able to get marvelously strong bacon, sprinkle each layer with a little salt.

Note: This terrine and its variations can be made half size, in a 4-cup mold or terrine. The container should be as deep as possible, to make at least four layers. If a loaf pan is used, a good size is the 5-cup one, 8½ by 4½ by 2½ inches.

Terrine de Poulet et Jambon
Terrine of Chicken and Ham

A cousin of the preceding Terrine de Body, this loaf also needs thin bacon. Thinly sliced packaged bacon will do, but good bacon sliced paper thin by the butcher would be better. A special touch in this loaf is green peppercorns, *poivre vert*, hard to find but appearing these days in more and more specialty food shops. (McCormick packages them.) Don't let a lack of green peppercorns stop you from making the terrine, though; it will still be fine with plenty of freshly ground black pepper instead. With good salty ham and strong bacon there would be no need for salt, but since what you can buy is likely to be pretty bland, a light sprinkle of salt on each layer of chicken should not be amiss.

The ham should be very thinly sliced from a leftover baked ham, or sliced to order from a baked or boiled ham in a store. Already packaged sliced ham is not as good.

Although "rich" in a way, this terrine makes a wonderfully appetite-stimulating first course, well worth a fine white wine, such as a Corton Charlemagne or Meursault from Burgundy, or a Pouilly-Fuissé, and is not too heavy to be followed by a roast or even a succulent stew.

Served as a main course for luncheon or supper, it could be accompanied by Potatoes, Celery, or Onions in Cream Sauce* and by a

salad involving fresh fruit, such as Orange and Cucumber* or grapefruit and endive. Lots of good crusty bread, the terrine, the salad,
and a Brie or Camembert cheese would make a fine meal without
anything else. In this case a light red wine such as a Santenay,
Beaune, or Volnay would go well with the terrine and also com-
plement the cheese.

Cook one day, serve the next, or up to four days later. Keep well
wrapped in foil and refrigerated until used.

For 5-cup loaf pan (8½″ x 4½″ x 2½″) or terrine

>   2 whole raw chicken breasts, skinned and boned
>   ½ pound cooked ham, thinly sliced
> ½–¾ pound thinly sliced bacon
>
>   2 tablespoons minced shallots (*or the white part of scallions*)
>   *per layer*
>   2 tablespoons finely chopped fresh parsley *per layer*
>   ⅛ teaspoon thyme *per layer*
>   ⅛ teaspoon savory *per layer*
>   ¼ of a large bay leaf, crumbled, *per layer*
>   6–8 green peppercorns *per layer or* several grinds of the pepper
>   mill
>   Sprinkle of salt *per layer*, unless ham and/or bacon are very
>   salty
>   ¼ teaspoon unflavored gelatin *per layer*
>
>   2 tablespoons Cognac
>   ¼ cup dry white wine, more or less, to come just below the
>   top of the loaf when loaf is pressed

2 tablespoons chopped parsley
   Parsley sprigs or watercress to garnish

Remove the center tendon between each pair of breasts and, with a small sharp knife, slice each thick portion horizontally at least once, twice if possible. With a rolling pin or the edge of a bread board, pound the slices and scraps between two pieces of waxed paper to make them as thin as possible. The idea is to make layers of bacon, chicken, ham, and seasonings, starting and ending with bacon. If the chicken is thin enough, it should make four layers, even if some are rather skimpy.

Divide the chicken and ham into four portions. Line the bottom of a small 5-cup loaf pan with bacon, to cover without too much overlapping. The amount will vary according to the thickness and width of the slices, but whatever it is, divide the rest into four more portions of the same amount. Cover the bacon with chicken, filling in the spaces between the larger slices with the lacy scraps. Cover the chicken with ham, making the layer evenly thick. Sprinkle the ham evenly with the shallots, parsley, thyme, savory, bay leaf, green peppercorns or freshly ground black pepper, salt (if the ham and/or bacon is not too strong), and gelatin. Repeat the layers—bacon, chicken, ham, seasonings, and gelatin—and top with the final layer of bacon.

Pour the Cognac over the top, and slowly pour the white wine in down the side of the loaf, until it can be seen just below the top layer of bacon when loaf is pressed with the fingers. Seal the pan with foil and place in a larger, shallow pan, with hot water poured in it to come halfway up the side of the loaf pan. Place in a pre-heated 325° oven and cook for 1¼ hours, or until the loaf has shrunk from the sides, the fat around it is clear, and a metal skewer goes in easily and comes out clean. Take the loaf out of the oven, loosen the foil, and put a brick or some heavy canned goods in a smaller pan on top. Do not pour off juices. Allow to cool and, when it is cool, refrigerate overnight, with the weight still on top.

To serve, remove the brick, the foil, and the solidified fat from the top of the loaf. To unmold, run a knife around the edge of the loaf and immerse the pan in an inch or so of hot water for a second or two. Invert a platter over the pan and then reverse, giving a slight jerk to dislodge the loaf. Spoon the jellied juices from each end over the loaf, sprinkle with finely chopped fresh parsley, wipe the platter, and surround with parsley sprigs or watercress. A cake knife or wide spatula helps in the serving of the layered slices. Yields about 14 half-inch slices.

Terrine de Veau, Porc, et Foie de Porc
Veal, Pork, and Pork Liver Terrine

Liver makes an interesting accent in this terrine, both visually and in the taste, and beef liver will do if pork liver is unavailable. The filler is flour rather than cereal, and an important seasoning is a favorite ingredient in French pâtés, Quatre-Épices.* The four-spice combination is made in the blender; the recipe given makes about ¾ cup, enough for a good many pâtés. It keeps well, like any other spice, in a tightly sealed jar. For those who do not want to make the spice in quantity, the spices are given separately in the amounts required for the recipe.

Served as a first course, the pâté can be followed by practically anything, simple or complicated. For a buffet, it can be surrounded by any of the good things suggested for the pâtés de campagne or pâtés maison. As a main course for luncheon or supper, Potatoes in Cream Sauce* and a salad with lots of crisp raw vegetables in it would be good, or a cheese soufflé and Ratatouille.* For a cold luncheon or supper, Salade Niçoise au Riz* and asparagus or artichokes with oil and vinegar would go well with the pâté. Any of the young red wines suggested for other veal and pork pâtés go with it, or a Muscadet or Pinot Chardonnay Mâcon if you prefer white, and a rosé would be fine when the pâté is served as a main course.

This terrine can be served the day after cooking, or up to a week later. It improves with keeping, well wrapped and refrigerated.

For 8-cup loaf pan (9" x 5" x 3") or terrine

- 1 pound ground veal
- 1 pound ground shoulder pork
- 1 pound pork liver *or* beef liver
- 2 tablespoons butter

- ¼ cup finely chopped shallots *or* onion
- ½ cup dry white wine *or* dry Vermouth

- 1 egg
- ¼ cup flour
- 1½ teaspoons Quatre-Épices* *or* 1 teaspoon white pepper, and ⅛ teaspoon each ground cloves, ground ginger, ground nutmeg
- 2 cloves garlic, chopped
- 1 tablespoon salt
- ½ teaspoon thyme
- ¼ teaspoon winter savory, crumbled, *or* ⅛ teaspoon rosemary, crumbled, and ⅛ teaspoon summer savory
- 2 tablespoons finely chopped fresh parsley
- ¼ cup Cognac

- ¾ pound bacon
- 2 bay leaves

- 2 tablespoons parsley
- Parsley sprigs or watercress

Put the veal and pork in a large mixing bowl. Trim membranes from the liver and cut into ¼- to ½-inch dice. Heat the butter in a skillet and cook the liver until it is light brown. Add the liver and juices from the pan to the meat in the mixing bowl.

In a very small saucepan, cook the shallots or onion in the wine until it has reduced by half. Add to the meat mixture.

In a small bowl, lightly beat the egg and mix with the flour until smooth. Using a strong fork, mash the garlic with the salt until there are no large pieces of garlic visible. Add, with the Quatre-Épices, thyme, savory, and parsley, to the egg and flour mixture. Add the Cognac and mix well. Add the mixture to the meats and mix thoroughly, using the hands if necessary to blend well.

Line an 8-cup loaf pan with bacon by laying some first on the bottom, then pressing strips along the sides (they will adhere long enough for the loaf to be put in) and then at the ends, with the excess hanging out, to be folded over the top. Pack the meat mixture into the pan, carefully pushing into corners and patting to avoid air holes. Bring the bacon over to cover. Add a little more if needed. Place the bay leaves on top and seal the pan with foil. Set in a larger, shallow pan with hot water poured in to come halfway up the side of the loaf pan. Set in preheated 325° oven and cook for 2 hours.

Remove from the oven and loosen foil around the edges. Do not pour off juices. Weight the loaf with a brick, or a smaller pan with canned goods in it. This presses the fat out and makes the loaf firm for slicing. You might want to pour out the water from the larger pan and set the loaf pan in it to catch any overflow from the loaf. When the loaf has cooled to room temperature, refrigerate, with the weight still on, 8 hours or overnight.

Remove weight, foil, and bay leaves. Unmold by running a knife around the edge, holding the pan briefly in a basin of hot water, and turning out onto a cold platter. Scrape off and discard hardened fat without disturbing the bacon. Spoon any jellied or liquid juices over the loaf, and wipe the edge of the platter clean. Sprinkle with parsley and surround with parsley sprigs or watercress. Yields about 30 quarter-inch slices.

Terrine de Veau et Porc
Veal and Pork Terrine

This is a rich and firm terrine which can serve a great many people. Filling an average 8-cup loaf pan to the brim, it yields 16 or so half-inch slices that can be cut into four pieces each, to be served on small rounds of French bread for a cocktail party hors-d'oeuvre. A more comfortable pan for the loaf is the 10-cup one, about 10 inches long, 5 inches wide, and 4 inches deep (see Introduction). The terrine can also, of course, be served for the first course in the conventional way, in quarter-inch slices on small plates with French bread, before practically anything. Like many pâtés, it makes a fine main course for luncheon or supper, and, as with all pâtés, a chunk makes an unusual and welcome hostess gift if you are not able to use it all yourself during its week or so of life.

With the Champagne Punch* or Red Wine Punch,* the terrine could be part of a fine buffet, sharing the table with other good things that are easy to buy or to prepare ahead, such as smoked salmon with cucumber in Sour Cream and Dill Sauce;* Grated Carrot Salad* or cold asparagus in Vinaigrette Dressing;* Pâté de Foies de Volaille (page 40) or Chopped Chicken Livers, Jewish Style (page 42); something hot in a chafing dish (macaroni and cheese, a vegetable in Cream Sauce,* Rice Pilaf with Almonds* or Scalloped Potatoes* in a big casserole); radishes, black olives, and celery on a bed of watercress; small sour gherkins or 2-inch pieces of scallion with the ends split, crisped for an hour in ice and water; a tray of cheeses; a great basket of good breads and thin dry toast—and dessert could be just fresh fruit or an assortment of store-bought French pastry.

The terrine should be made one day and served the next, or up to a week later. It improves with keeping, well wrapped and re-frigerated.

For 8-cup loaf pan (9" x 5" x 3") or terrine

1½ pounds ground veal
1½ pounds ground pork shoulder
 ½ cup uncooked oatmeal
  1 cup chopped celery
 ½ cup finely chopped fresh parsley
 ¼ cup pine nuts (optional)

  1 egg
 ⅓ cup Cognac
  3 cloves garlic, chopped
  1 tablespoon salt
 ½ teaspoon freshly ground black pepper
 ½ teaspoon marjoram
 ½ teaspoon rosemary, finely crumbled
 ½ teaspoon thyme
 ½ teaspoon nutmeg

 ¾ pound bacon
  2 bay leaves

  2 tablespoons chopped parsley
     Parsley sprigs or watercress to garnish

Put the veal and pork, oatmeal, celery, parsley, and nuts, if used, in a large mixing bowl. Mix lightly.

In a small bowl, lightly beat the egg and add the Cognac. Using a strong fork, mash the garlic with the salt until there are no large pieces. Add, with the pepper, marjoram, rosemary, thyme, and nutmeg, to the egg and Cognac mixture. Mix thoroughly with the ingredients in the large mixing bowl, using the hands if necessary to blend well.

Line an 8-cup loaf pan with bacon by laying some first on the bottom, then pressing strips along the sides (they will adhere long enough for the loaf to be put in), and then at the ends, with the excess hanging out, to be folded over the top. Pack the meat mixture into the pan, carefully pushing into corners and patting to avoid air holes. Bring the bacon over to cover. Add a little more if needed. Place the bay leaves on top and seal the pan with foil. Set in a larger shallow pan with hot water poured in to come halfway up the side of the loaf pan. Place in preheated 325° oven and cook for 2 hours.

Remove from the oven and loosen foil around the edges. Do not pour off juices. Weight the loaf with a brick or another loaf pan with canned goods in it. This presses out the fat and makes the loaf firm for slicing. You might want to pour the water out of the larger shallow pan and set the loaf pan in it to catch any overflow from the loaf. When the loaf has come to room temperature, refrigerate 8 hours or overnight.

Remove weight, foil, and bay leaves. Unmold by running a knife around the edge, holding the pan briefly in a basin of hot water, and inverting onto a cold platter. Scrape off and discard hardened fat without disturbing the bacon. Spoon any jellied or liquid juices over the loaf and wipe the edge of the platter clean. Sprinkle with parsley, surround with parsley sprigs or watercress, and serve in quarter-inch individual slices, or in half-inch slices cut in four, each quarter on a square of toast or round of French bread. Yields about 30 quarter-inch slices or 16 half-inch slices.

Terrine de Veau et Porc au Jambon
Terrine of Veal, Pork, and Ham

This terrine has the classic addition of little strips of meat, marinated in seasoned Cognac and buried in the loaf. They add flavor and make an attractive pattern in the slices. In this case, the strips are veal and ham. They could also be veal and tongue, or veal and pork, or half one of the meats and half fresh pork fat. Pork fat makes a nice white accent in the slices and is often found in French pâtés and terrines. The ham can be leftovers from a baked ham, a slice of good delicatessen boiled or baked ham, or part of a fully cooked ham steak, trimmed of fat and bone.

Served as first course, luncheon or supper main course, buffet, or picnic, this loaf is versatile enough to go with or before the things suggested for other veal- and pork-based loaves. It is up to a good red wine—a Beaujolais Brouilly or Juliénas, a Volnay or Beaune—or a simple Zinfandel or Gamay from California.

Use it the day after making it, or up to a week later. It improves with keeping, well wrapped and refrigerated.

For 8-cup loaf pan (9" x 5" x 3") or terrine

¼ pound veal, ¼ inch thick, in ¼-inch strips
¼ pound cooked ham, ¼ inch thick, in ¼-inch strips
½ cup Cognac
¼ cup finely chopped shallots *or* onion
¼ cup finely chopped fresh parsley
    Pinch each of allspice, thyme, salt, pepper

1¼ pounds ground veal
1¼ pounds ground pork shoulder

 2 eggs
¼ cup flour
2½ teaspoons salt
½ teaspoon freshly ground black pepper
 1 teaspoon marjoram
¼ teaspoon rosemary, finely crumbled
⅛ teaspoon thyme
 1 small bay leaf, finely crumbled

¾ pound bacon

 2 tablespoons chopped parsley
    Parsley or watercress to garnish

Put the veal and ham strips in a small nonmetallic bowl. Pour the Cognac over the meat strips and add the shallots, parsley, and pinches of seasonings. Cover and allow to stand (marinate) for 1 to 2 hours, stirring occasionally.

Put the ground veal and pork in a large mixing bowl and mix lightly.

In another small bowl, lightly beat the eggs and add the flour to make a smooth mixture. Add the salt, pepper, marjoram, rosemary, thyme, and bay leaf. Mix well and add to the ground meats. Mix thoroughly until the mixture is light and has absorbed some of the moisture.

Pick out the strips of meat from the bowl where they have been marinating and set aside. Add all the marinade juices and solids to the ground meat mixture. Mix well.

Line an 8-cup loaf pan with bacon by laying some first on the bottom, then pressing strips along the sides (they will adhere long enough for the meat to be put in), then at the ends, with the excess hanging out, to be folded over the loaf. Put a third of the ground meat mixture into the pan, carefully pushing it into corners and patting to avoid air holes. Place half the marinated strips lengthwise on top, cover with another third of the ground meat, then the other half of the strips, and top with the last of the ground meat mixture. Bring up the overhanging bacon to cover, adding a little more if needed. Seal the pan with foil. Set in a larger shallow pan with hot water to come halfway up the side of the loaf pan. Place in preheated 350° oven and cook for 1½ hours.

Remove from the oven and loosen foil around the edges. Do not pour off juices. Weight the loaf with a brick or a smaller pan with canned goods in it. This presses out fat and makes the loaf firm for slicing. You might want to pour the water out of the large shallow pan and set the loaf pan in it to catch any overflow from the loaf. When the loaf has come to room temperature, refrigerate for 8 hours or overnight with weight still on.

Terrine de Veau et Porc au Jambon / 81

To unmold, remove weight and foil, run a knife around the edge of the loaf, hold the pan briefly in a basin of hot water, and turn out upside down onto a cold platter. Scrape off and discard any hardened fat without disturbing the bacon. Spoon any jellied or liquid juices from platter or pan over the loaf and wipe the edges of the platter clean. Sprinkle with chopped parsley, surround with parsley sprigs or watercress, and serve in quarter-inch slices. Yields about 30 slices.

Terrine de Veau au Bacon
Veal and Bacon Loaf

The Canadian bacon in this veal loaf adds a delicate touch of ham flavor and, with the diced pork fat, makes a little random pattern in the pink slices. The whole thing is rather delicate and is particularly good preceding a main course of chicken, a baked fish, or a seafood casserole, but it would also be good before something as hearty as a roast or a veal stew.

As a main-course luncheon or supper dish, it should be accompanied by something that won't overwhelm it, a vegetable in Cream Sauce,* asparagus with Hollandaise sauce, or a cheese soufflé for something hot; lettuce, sliced tomatoes, and hard-cooked eggs with mayonnaise for something cold. Even more simply, it could be served with just a leafy salad, crusty bread, cheese, and fruit.

A fine white wine from Burgundy would go well with this pâté—such as a five-year-old estate-bottled Corton or Meursault—but lighter, cheaper whites like California Chardonnay or Sauvignon Blanc would be good too. For a red, an eight- or ten-year-old Bordeaux in the expensive category; an Italian Bardolino or California Pinot Noir for a less expensive one.

Make the terrine one day, serve it the next, or up to a week later. It improves with keeping, well wrapped in foil and refrigerated.

For 5-cup loaf pan (8½" x 4½" x 2½") or terrine

1½ pounds ground veal
 ¼ pound fresh pork fat, loin or fresh-ham fat, in ¼-inch cubes
 ¼ pound Canadian bacon, in ¼-inch cubes
 ¼ cup finely chopped shallots *or* onion
  2 tablespoons finely chopped fresh parsley
 ¼ cup Madeira

  1 egg
  2 tablespoons flour
 ¼ cup heavy cream
1¼ teaspoons salt
 ½ teaspoon freshly ground black pepper
 ⅛ teaspoon ground ginger
 ⅛ teaspoon mace
 ⅛ teaspoon rosemary, crumbled
 ½ teaspoon thyme
 ½ bay leaf, finely crumbled

 ¾ pound bacon

  2 tablespoons chopped parsley
     Parsley sprigs or watercress to garnish

Combine the veal, pork fat, Canadian bacon, shallots or onion, parsley, and Madeira in a large mixing bowl.

In a small bowl, lightly beat the egg with the flour and stir in the cream and seasonings. Mix thoroughly with the contents of the large bowl, a little at a time, and beat with a wooden spoon until the mixture has dried out slightly.

If you have a blender, you can simplify this by blending quickly the egg, flour, Madeira, cream, seasonings, and a third of the veal, placing it with the rest of the ingredients in a large bowl, and mixing well.

Line a 5-cup loaf pan with bacon. Start with slices on the bottom, then press slices on the sides. They will adhere until meat mixture is put in. Finally, line the ends of the pan, allowing excess to hang over. Pack in the meat mixture, pressing into corners and patting to avoid air holes. Flatten the top and bring the hanging bacon over to cover. Use a little more if needed. Seal the pan with foil. Set in a larger shallow pan with hot water poured in to come halfway up the side of the loaf pan. Place in a preheated 350° oven and cook for 1¼ to 1½ hours or until juices run clear, not pink or opaque, when loaf is pricked and pressed.

Remove from the oven and loosen foil around the edges. Do not pour off juices. Weight the loaf with a brick or a smaller loaf pan with canned goods in it. (This is to press out the fat and make the loaf firm for slicing.) Pour the water out of the larger pan and set the weighted loaf in it to catch any overflow. When the loaf has come to room temperature, refrigerate for 8 hours or overnight, with weight still on.

Remove weight and foil. Unmold by running a knife around the edge of the loaf, holding the pan briefly in a basin of hot water, and turning out onto a cold platter. Scrape off and discard any hardened fat without disturbing bacon. Spoon any jellied or liquid juices from the pan or platter over the loaf and wipe the edge of the platter clean. Sprinkle with chopped parsley and surround with parsley or watercress. Serve in quarter-inch slices. Yields about 22 slices.

Terrine de Lapin
Rabbit Pâté

Full of taste and slightly gamy, this pâté should please those who are free of prejudice against rabbit and might very well help to overcome prejudice in others. Part of the secret is allowing the pâté mixture, with all its seasonings, to stand overnight and then letting it stand another night after it is cooked. In fact, it can stand for two nights before cooking and two or three days after cooking, before being served. It will keep for the usual week from the day of cooking, well covered and refrigerated.

Game pâtés like this one call for red wine. They are excellent with young fruity wines such as a good Beaujolais, but they also stand up to a big full wine like a fine St. Émilion from Bordeaux or a Cabernet Sauvignon from California. Served as a first course, they can be followed by something hearty to go with the same wine, even venison or wildfowl. Steak au Poivre, thick chops, or Coq au Vin Rouge would be good too, with parsleyed potatoes, a leafy salad, and a Brie or Taleggio cheese to follow, with fresh fruit or a cool sherbet to finish.

For 8-cup loaf pan (9" x 5" x 3") or terrine

2½ pounds trimmed ready-to-cook rabbit, fresh or frozen
1 medium onion, quartered
1 clove garlic, chopped
¾ pound ground veal
1 pound ground pork shoulder

¾ cup dry red wine
¼ cup Cognac
2¾ teaspoons salt
¼ teaspoon freshly ground black pepper
1 teaspoon thyme
2 tablespoons finely chopped fresh parsley
1 tablespoon olive oil

2 eggs
¼ cup flour
More dry red wine if needed to moisten

¾ pound bacon
1 bay leaf
4 parsley stems

Parsley sprigs or watercress to garnish

Thaw rabbit, if frozen, and remove all possible meat from the bones, cutting and scraping with a sharp knife. If desired, the liver can be lightly sautéed in butter, chopped, and added. Discard waste; you should have 2 cups (1 pound) of rabbit meat. Put the rabbit, onion, and garlic through the meat grinder, using medium blade. (If you have no grinder, finely chop the rabbit meat and onion and mince the garlic.) Mix with the ground veal and pork in a large mixing bowl.

In a small bowl mix wine, Cognac, salt, pepper, thyme, parsley, and oil. Add to the meat mixture and mix thoroughly. Cover and refrigerate overnight. (Salt is in the proportion of ¼ teaspoon per quarter pound [½ cup] of ground meat. If by any chance you have less than 1 pound [2 cups] of rabbit meat, reduce the salt accordingly. If there is just a little more, leave the salt the same.)

Next day, beat the eggs in a small bowl and mix in the flour to make a smooth paste. Add to the meat mixture and mix thoroughly. If mixture is very dry, add a little more wine for easier mixing.

Line an 8-cup loaf pan with bacon slices and pack in the meat mixture, pressing into corners and patting to avoid air holes. Cover with bacon slices and place the bay leaf and parsley stems on top. Seal pan with foil and place in a larger shallow pan with hot water to come halfway up the side of the loaf pan. Set in a preheated 325° oven and cook for 2½ hours.

Remove the pâté from the oven and allow it to cool undisturbed, without removing foil cover, until it is at room temperature, about 5 hours. Refrigerate, still covered, overnight, if possible for two nights.

To unmold, remove bay leaf and parsley stems, run a knife around the edge of the loaf, immerse pan in an inch or so of hot water for a few moments, and invert onto a platter. Serve sliced, surrounded by parsley sprigs or watercress. Yields about 15 half-inch slices.

Terrine de Caneton Le Chambertin
Duck Terrine

From Le Chambertin, a delightful French restaurant in New York, comes this classic terrine of duck. Since it involves boning, it could hardly be called an easy terrine to make, but the triumphant result is worth the effort. (At least in this case the skin does not have to be kept intact, as it does for a galantine.) With a really good sharp knife and patience, it is not too difficult, and you will acquire a familiarity with the bird's anatomy that will come in handy when you tackle a galantine of duck or chicken.

A perfect first-course terrine, it can be served on a lettuce leaf with the usual *cornichons*, or sour gherkins, or, since oranges have such an affinity for duck, with wedges of orange. As a main-course luncheon or supper dish, it is well complemented by an Orange and Cucumber Salad,* followed by soft cheeses like Brie or Camembert or a goat cheese and, of course, plenty of crusty bread.

To celebrate the source of the restaurant's name, the wine could be an estate-bottled Chambertin, which would be superb (and expensive), but a less grand red Burgundy, like a good Beaujolais or Mâcon, or a Rhône, like a Côte Rôtie or Hermitage, would also be excellent.

This terrine can be served the day after cooking, but it is better two days to one week later. Keep it well wrapped in foil and refrigerated until used.

For 8-cup loaf pan (9" x 5" x 3") or terrine

   1 duckling, 5–6 pounds

¼ pound lean cooked ham, diced
  5 slices fat bacon, diced
¼ teaspoon thyme
¼ teaspoon salt
⅛ teaspoon freshly ground black pepper
¼ cup Madeira *or* Cognac

¼ pound ground veal
¼ pound ground lean pork
½ pound fresh pork fat (from loin or fresh ham)

  2 eggs
½ teaspoon allspice
  1 teaspoon thyme
1½ teaspoons salt
½ teaspoon freshly ground black pepper
¼ cup marc *or* Cognac

  1 tablespoon butter
¾–1 pound fresh pork fat (from loin or fresh ham) in thin sheets

    Parsley sprigs or watercress to garnish

Place the duck on its breast and slit the skin down the back from
the neck to the tail. Starting at the neck, pull back the skin at one
side and, with a very sharp pointed knife, cut the skin away from
the meat until the back is all exposed. Cut off the wings and legs,
skin and all. Remove and reserve the breast skin, detaching it care-

fully from the center breast cartilage. Keep breast skin, in one large piece if possible, to serve as a cover for the loaf. (If it has to be cut up to remove, the loaf can be covered with overlapping strips.)

Remove the breast meat in slices as large as possible. Pat them dry and place them in a bowl with the diced ham and bacon, thyme, salt, pepper, and Madeira or Cognac. Allow this to stand for at least 2 hours to marinate, stirring occasionally.

Remove skin from the legs and wings and cut and scrape off the meat. Cut and scrape all remaining meat from carcass. Discard carcass, reserving duck liver. If you have a meat grinder, grind all this duck meat with the veal, pork, and pork fat, using the medium blade. Without a grinder, finely chop the duck meat and pork fat and mix with the other meats.

In a small bowl, beat the eggs and add the rest of the seasonings, and the marc or Cognac. Add to the ground meat mixture a little at a time, mixing thoroughly after each addition. Pat the liver dry, cut in small pieces, sauté briefly and quickly in a tablespoon of butter, and add to the meat mixture.

Remove the breast meat from the marinade, pat dry, and reserve. Add the ham and bacon dice and the marinade juices to the meat mixture.

Line an 8-cup loaf pan with the fat pork sheets. If the fat is too thick and not in large enough sheets, pound between sheets of waxed paper with a rolling pin or the edge of a bread board, to spread it out and weld pieces together. Pack half the meat mixture into the lined pan, spread the breast pieces on top, and cover with the rest of the meat mixture. Cover the loaf with reserved skin from the breast. Cover the pan with foil and place in a larger shallow pan with hot water to come halfway up the side of the loaf pan. Place in a preheated 400° oven 1¼ to 1½ hours, or until loaf has shrunk from the sides and fat runs clear around it when it is pricked and pressed.

Remove from the oven, loosen foil, and place a brick or smaller weighted loaf pan on top. This is to press out the fat and make the loaf firm and sliceable. When thoroughly cool, refrigerate overnight with the weight still on.

To unmold, remove duck skin or pork fat from the top of the loaf. Run a knife around the edge, dip the pan briefly in an inch or so of hot water, and reverse onto a platter. Remove lardlike solidified fat, but save any meat juices that cling to it to serve with the loaf. Serve in slices, on a platter, surrounded by parsley or watercress. Yields about 15 half-inch slices.

GALANTINES

For pure glamour there is nothing like a galantine of duck or chicken. There is the bird in its original shape, with drumsticks and wings in place, attractively decorated under a glaze and surrounded by glittering chopped aspic, ready to be cut right down the middle to reveal solid pâté.

A galantine is defined as boned poultry or meat, stuffed with its own and/or other meats, sewn up and cooked in stock, then cooled, decorated with aspic, and served cold. The decoration can be a simple coating of clear aspic or the more complicated and exciting one given here, with clear aspic applied over a base coating of creamy-white aspic (Chaud-Froid) on which vegetable decorations have been placed. Traditionally, all bones are removed and, in the case of a bird, all meat removed from the skin, the skin then forming a package for the pâté mixture. (When it is meat, such as breast or shoulder of veal, the pâté is rolled up in the boned meat or stuffed into a pocket cut in the meat.) But in the next two recipes, the birds are not completely boned; the drumsticks and second-joint wing bones are left intact, and we don't worry if a little meat remains attached to the skin. This makes it possible to reconstruct the bird so that it almost looks as though no bones have been removed at all.

Another departure in these recipes from the classic French way of preparing a galantine is that the stock is flavored with scallions and fresh ginger rather than the customary carrot, onion, celery, and parsley. Both ways are given, though, in case fresh ginger is unavailable.

The ham used in the recipes should be leftovers from a baked ham, a slice of good delicatessen boiled or baked ham, or a piece cut from a fully cooked ham steak, trimmed of fat and bone.

To produce the triumph that is called a galantine, you have to allow a minimum of three days, sometimes as many as five. Not all of this time is preparation, of course; most of it is waiting time while the pâté marinates before cooking and rests to develop its flavors afterward. As for the work involved, since it is spread over three days or so, you have time to recover after each step. By the time it is served, the effort is long behind you and you are free to enjoy it with your guests. Actually, it is an interesting job to do, and unquestionably rewarding.

Galantine de Canard
Boned Stuffed Duck

Allow three to four days from the start of preparation to the time of serving. First day: bone duck and prepare ingredients for marinating; marinate overnight, preferably two nights. Second or third day: stuff galantine, cook, cool, and refrigerate overnight. Third or fourth day: make aspics and decorate galantine. Serve that day if there is time for chilling, or up to five days later.

Although the galantine, like any pâté, is a fine first course, it seems a pity not to make it the star of the show. It could be the focus of a buffet, with a variety of other things to go with it, one of them, perhaps, a hot chafing-dish vegetable. A few suggestions: a bowl of cold shrimp with a Green Sauce* dip, hard-cooked eggs with mayonnaise, Grated Carrot Salad* or Celery Root Rémoulade,* Hot Potato Salad* (still good when it cools), *cornichons* (little sour gherkins), a big tray of cheeses, and the accompanying crusty bread. The chafing-dish vegetable could be Celery in Cream Sauce* or sautéed mushrooms, and dessert could be simply fresh fruit or a rich store-bought cake, with coffee and Cognac or Champagne to finish.

Needless to say, the entire galantine does not have to be used at one time. It is nice to present it whole for the first serving, but leftovers can be carefully wrapped in foil, to preserve the decorations, and refrigerated for use up to a week after cooking.

This most elegant of pâtés is good even with simple young red wines like Beaujolais or California Zinfandel, but is worthy of a great red Bordeaux from St. Émilion or Pomerol too. Also good would be a Champagne Punch* or Red Wine Punch.*

1 five-pound duck, boned, bones reserved (page 105)

   Slices of breast meat from duck
   Liver of duck, in ½-inch pieces
¼ pound cooked ham in ⅜-inch dice
 4 slices fat bacon, diced
¼ cup minced shallots *or* white part of scallions
1–2 quarter-inch-diced truffles and juice (optional)

1 teaspoon minced orange rind (no white)
½ teaspoon salt
⅛ teaspoon freshly ground black pepper
⅛ teaspoon Quatre-Épices* or allspice
¼ cup Port

  Thigh meat, first joint wing meat, and scraps of meat from
  duck carcass
¾ pound ground pork shoulder
¾ pound ground veal

1 egg
2 teaspoons salt
½ teaspoon freshly ground black pepper
½ teaspoon thyme
½ teaspoon marjoram
½ teaspoon Quatre-Épices* or allspice
¼ cup Cognac
½ cup dry white wine

  Poaching Stock (page 106)
¼ cup pistachio nuts, shelled and peeled

4 large scallions, with green tops, cut across in two
3 slices fresh ginger, about 1-inch diameter and ⅟₁₆-inch thick, *or*
  1 carrot (scraped), 1 stalk of celery with leaves, 2 or 3 parsley
  sprigs, and a pinch of thyme
10 whole black peppercorns
6–8 cups ready-to-use canned chicken broth, or
  enough to cover duck

1–2 oranges, unpeeled and thinly sliced
  Parsley sprigs

Spread out the duck skin, outer side down, in a nonmetallic bowl or baking dish with the wings and drumsticks hanging over the edge. In the middle of the skin, where the carcass was, put the slices of breast meat, cut-up liver, ham, bacon, shallots or scallions, and truffles (if used). Sprinkle with the orange rind, salt, pepper, spice mixture, and Port. Fold the legs and wings and surrounding skin over all this, cover with foil or plastic, and refrigerate overnight or as long as two days.

Grind or finely chop all remaining bits of boned duck meat, trimming off fat and tendons. Mix with the ground pork and veal in a large mixing bowl.

In a small bowl, lightly beat the egg, add the seasonings and the Cognac, and mix thoroughly with the ground meats. Add the white wine, a little at a time, and continue mixing until all is well blended. This may be done in the blender, at least partially: put the egg and seasonings directly into the blender and add a cup or so of the meats. Give it a short whirl and add another cup of meat, using the white wine to moisten. The blender jar will have to be scraped down periodically. Blend as much of the meat as possible. If it can't all be blended, just mix the leftovers with the blender contents; a little change of texture doesn't hurt. Put the now well-mixed meat and seasonings in a nonmetallic bowl, cover with foil or plastic, and refrigerate, as with the skin and its contents, overnight or up to two days.

Make the poaching stock, cool to room temperature, and refrigerate.

When you are ready to cook the galantine, remove stock and meats from the refrigerator. Separate and discard solidified fat from the stock. Put the stock and its solids into a large kettle or enameled ironware casserole, preferably oval, that will take the galantine and wing and thigh bones snugly, deep enough to allow for the broth which will be added to the stock to cover it all.

Open the envelope of skin and pick out the breast slices and truffles (if used) and set them aside. Spoon the liver, ham, bacon, shallots, etc., out of the skin and add, with the marinade juices, to the ground meats. Add the nuts and mix to distribute evenly through the mixture.

Now the skin is to be stuffed, the ground meat mixture and the breast slices occupying the space where the carcass was. Spread out the skin, outer side down, and put half the meat mixture in. Sprinkle with half the truffles (if used), cover with the breast slices, sprinkle with the rest of the truffles, and top with the rest of the ground meat. Bring up the skin on each side, and sew it together with white thread with no knots at either end so it can be removed easily later. Fold the flap of neck skin up and sew it to the back. Pat and gently press the duck into shape, with the drumsticks and wings in their proper places.

Spread out a large piece of dampened cheesecloth in several layers, and place the duck in the center at one end. Roll it up firmly, twisting and squeezing the ends as you go, to keep the duck in shape. Tie the ends close to the bird.

Place the wrapped duck, breast side up, in the kettle or casserole with the poaching stock and its solids. Add the scallions, ginger, peppercorns, and canned chicken broth to cover. If the bird floats above the liquid, weight it with a heatproof plate or saucer. Bring to a boil, reduce heat, and simmer, partially covered, for 1½ hours. Turn breast side down and cool in the stock. Remove from the stock and take off the cheesecloth. Refrigerate overnight, wrapped in foil.

Remove grease from the stock (chilling the stock first helps) and strain through a sieve lined with layers of dampened cheesecloth. Discard solids. Measure 4 cups of strained stock with which to make Chaud-Froid and aspic, and refrigerate overnight. (You may reserve any leftover stock for other uses.)

Next day, heat stock to liquefy. Prepare Chaud-Froid, aspic, and vegetables for decoration (pages 107 to 110).

To decorate place the duck on a piece of foil or waxed paper and carefully remove any visible threads with tweezers. Leave any that resist or can't be easily reached, to remove when slices are served. Turn breast side up and wipe gently with paper towels to remove some of the fat, which could keep the aspic from sticking.

With the galantine chilled, and the Chaud-Froid cool but not setting, brush on the first coat of Chaud-Froid with a pastry brush. This first coat may have to be rubbed on. Refrigerate for a few minutes to set. When it has set, brush on another thin even coat, covering all visible parts, including drumstick ends and wings. Chill for a few minutes. Continue to apply the white aspic with a spoon or brush, chilling after each coat, until all skin is well masked by sauce. Set white aspic container in a bowl of hot water if it tends to get too firm during this process, which can take about an hour. Before the last coat sets, put the decorations in place with tweezers or the tip of a sharp knife, and chill to set. When the decorations are firmly set in the white aspic, bring 1 cup of the Clear Aspic to the consistency of egg whites by setting it in its container in a basin of ice and water and stirring until it reaches the desired stage. Carefully spoon a thin layer over the entire bird to form a transparent glaze. Chill to set. Return leftover Clear Aspic to the rest and chill to chop and serve around the galantine. (For quick setting, heat the aspic to liquefy and pour into a cake pan to chill.)

To serve, slide the duck off the paper or foil onto a platter. Chop the Clear Aspic and surround the galantine with it. Add some overlapping thin slices of orange on each side of the platter, and tuck a few sprigs of parsley around, close to the bird. Carve down the middle lengthwise, turn each half cut side down, and carve slices from the part between wing and drumstick. (Wings and drumsticks have a delicate flavor of their own and can be served too.) Serves 16 to 18 as a first course or part of a buffet.

Galantine de Poularde
Boned Stuffed Chicken

Allow three days from the start of preparation to the time of serving. First day: bone chicken and prepare ingredients for marinating; marinate overnight. Second day: stuff galantine, cook, cool, and refrigerate overnight. Third day: make aspics and decorate galantine. Serve that day if there is time for chilling, or up to five days later.

This galantine is probably best served, at least the first time around, as the main item in a buffet, as suggested for the duck galantine which precedes this recipe. A few alternate ideas for the rest of the

buffet are Pâté de Foies de Volaille; Potatoes in Cream Sauce*
for the chafing dish; raw mushroom salad; cooked green beans or
asparagus in Vinaigrette Dressing;* deviled eggs; a bowl of watercress, scallions, and celery; Cumberland Sauce* for the galantine
instead of pickles; a tray of cheeses; and a basket of thin dry toast
and crusty bread.

It's hard to decide what is best to drink with this subtle magnifi-
cence—an Extra-Sec Champagne, a fine château-bottling from Bordeaux, an estate-bottling from Burgundy, or some young and fruity
wine, like a Beaujolais Moulin-à-Vent or Chiroubles, or a white like
a Pouilly-Fuissé.

1 roasting chicken, 3½ pounds, boned

Slices of breast meat
¼ pound cooked ham *or* tongue, in ¼–½-inch cubes
1 quarter-inch diced truffle and juice (optional)
¼ teaspoon salt
¼ teaspoon freshly ground black pepper
¼ teaspoon thyme
¼ cup Cognac

Thigh meat, first joint wing meat, and scraps of meat from
the carcass
½ pound ground veal
½ pound pork sausage, casings (if any) removed
1 clove garlic, minced
2 tablespoons minced shallots *or* onion
¼ cup white wine
2 tablespoons Madeira

1 egg
1 teaspoon salt
¼ teaspoon freshly ground black pepper
⅛ teaspoon nutmeg
¼ teaspoon thyme
⅛ teaspoon savory, crumbled
½ bay leaf, finely crumbled
   Poaching Stock (see page 106)

¼ cup pistachio nuts, shelled and peeled

4 large scallions, with green tops, cut across in two
3 slices fresh ginger, about 1 inch in diameter and $\frac{1}{16}$ inch thick,
  or 1 carrot (scraped), 1 stalk of celery with leaves, 2 or 3 parsley
  sprigs, and a pinch of thyme
10 peppercorns
6–8 cups ready-to-use chicken broth, or enough to cover chicken

Spread out the chicken skin, outside down, in a nonmetallic bowl
or baking dish with the wings and drumsticks hanging over the
edge. In the middle of the skin where the carcass was, put the
breast slices, ham or tongue cubes, and optional truffle with juice.
Sprinkle with the salt, pepper, and thyme, and pour in the Cognac.
Fold the legs, wings, and surrounding skin over all this, cover with
foil or plastic, and refrigerate overnight.

Finely chop or grind all remaining pieces of chicken meat, removing any tendons. Place in a large mixing bowl with the ground veal,
crumbled sausage meat, garlic, shallots, wine, and Madeira. Mix
together.

In a small bowl, lightly beat the egg and add the seasonings—salt, pepper, nutmeg, thyme, savory, and bay leaf. Add to the meats in the large mixing bowl and mix thoroughly. Place in a nonmetallic bowl and refrigerate overnight, as with the skin and its contents.

Make the poaching stock, cool, and refrigerate.

When you are ready to cook the galantine, remove stock and meats from the refrigerator. Discard solidified fat from the stock. Put the stock and its solids into a large kettle or enameled ironware casserole, preferably oval, that will take the galantine snugly, deep enough to allow for the broth which will be added to the stock to cover the galantine.

Open the envelope of skin, pick out the breast slices and truffles, if used, and set them aside. Spoon the ham or tongue cubes out of the skin and add, with all the juices that go with them, to the ground meats. Add the nuts and stir the mixture to blend everything evenly.

Now the skin is to be stuffed, the ground meat mixture and the breast slices occupying the space where the carcass was. Spread out the skin, outer side down, and put half the meat mixture in. Sprinkle with half the truffles (if used), cover with breast slices, sprinkle with the rest of the truffles, and top with the rest of the meat mixture. Bring up the skin on each side and sew it together, with no knots at either end of the thread so it can be removed easily later. Fold the flap of neck skin up and tack it to the back. Pat and gently press the bird into shape, with the drumsticks and wings in their proper places.

Spread out a large piece of dampened cheesecloth in several layers, and place the chicken in the center at one end. Roll it up firmly, twisting and squeezing the ends as you go, to keep the galantine in a nice oval shape. Tie the ends close to the bird.

Place the wrapped chicken, breast side up, in the kettle or casserole with the poaching stock and its solids. Add the scallions, ginger, peppercorns, and canned chicken broth to cover. If it floats above the liquid, weight with a heatproof plate or saucer. Bring to a boil, reduce heat, and simmer, partially covered, for 1½ hours. Turn breast side down and cool in the stock. Remove from the stock and take off the cheesecloth. Refrigerate overnight, wrapped in foil.

Degrease the stock and strain through a sieve lined with layers of dampened cheesecloth. Discard solids. Measure 4 cups of the strained stock with which to make Chaud-Froid and aspic. Refrigerate overnight. Reserve any leftover stock for other uses.

Next day, heat stock to liquefy. Prepare Chaud-Froid, aspic, and vegetables for decoration (pages 107 to 110).

Place the chicken on a piece of foil or waxed paper and carefully remove threads with tweezers. Leave any that resist or can't be easily reached, to remove when slices are served. Turn breast side up and wipe gently with paper towels to remove some of the fat, which could keep the aspic from sticking.

With the galantine chilled, and the Chaud-Froid cool but not setting, brush on the first coat of Chaud-Froid with a pastry brush. This first coat may have to be rubbed on. Refrigerate for a few minutes to set. When it has set, brush on another thin, even coat, covering all visible parts, including drumstick bones and wings. Chill for a few minutes. Continue to apply the Chaud-Froid with a spoon or brush, chilling after each coat, until all skin is well masked by the sauce. Set Chaud-Froid container in a bowl of hot water if it tends to get too firm during this process, which may take an hour. Before the last coat sets, put the decorations (see Vegetable Designs, page 109) in place with tweezers or the tip of a sharp knife, and chill to set. When the decorations are firmly set in the Chaud-Froid, bring 1 cup of the Clear Aspic to the consistency of egg whites by setting it, in its container, in a basin of ice and water and stirring. Carefully spoon a thin layer over the entire bird to form a transparent glaze. Chill to set. Return leftover Clear Aspic to the rest and chill to chop and serve around the galantine. For quick setting, heat the aspic to liquefy and pour into a cake pan to chill.

To serve, slide the galantine off the paper onto a platter. Finely chop the clear aspic and surround the galantine with it. Tuck a few sprigs of parsley around, close to the bird. Carve down the middle lengthwise, turn one half cut-side down, and carve slices from the part between wing and drumstick. Wings and drumsticks have a delicate flavor of their own and can be served too. Serves 8 to 10 as a first course or part of a buffet.

Supplementary Instructions for Galantines
How to Bone Poultry

Cut off wing tips and set aside, with neck and giblets, for the stock. Set the bird, breast side down, on a cutting board. Using a small sharp knife, make a cut through the skin, to the bone, from neck to tail. Starting at the neck area, free the skin around the shoulders, turning it back to expose the part where the wing is joined to the carcass. This can be done with the fingers. Move the wing bone to find out where the joint is, and cut the flesh to expose the ball joint. Sever the joint to free the wing bone from the carcass. Do the same with the other wing.

Separate the skin from the wing bones up to the next joint, using the fingers as much as possible and the knife when needed. When you use the knife, cut some flesh with the skin rather than risk making a hole in the skin by trying to remove it without any flesh adhering. Find the next joint and cut through at the ball joint to free the meaty wing bone, leaving the next wing bone still in the skin and attached to the rest of the skin. Set aside the two meaty wing bones.

Stand the bird on its tail and, with the fingers, separate the skin from the breast meat and the sides, down to the beginning of the thighs. Cut the skin carefully from the breast bone (it is thin here) and turn it back. Lay the bird down again and detach the thigh bone from the carcass at the joint. Separate the skin from the thigh bone, using the fingers as much as possible, cutting to include some flesh when necessary. Find and cut through the next joint of the leg, leaving the drumstick intact, with its skin on, and still attached to the rest of the skin. Set aside the thigh bone.

Cut the skin away from the lower back to the tail, leaving the tail attached to the skin. Free the rest of the carcass with fingers and knife. Lift out the carcass and set aside. Spread out the skin, flesh side down, and sew up any holes with a needle and coarse white thread. Do not knot the thread, and leave a bit at each end of the mend for easy removal later. Sew up, in the same way, any excessive tears around the neck and tail.

Cut the breast meat from the carcass in slices as large as possible. Cut and scrape all the rest of the meat from the carcass and the severed wing and thigh bones, discarding fat and tendons. Reserve bones and carcass, with neck and giblets, for the stock. Proceed with the recipe.

Poaching Stock for Poultry Galantines

Put neck, gizzard, heart, liver (if not used in loaf), carcass bones broken up, wing tips, thigh, and first-joint wing bones from the boned bird in a large kettle or enameled ironware pot. Add 2 quarts water and ½ teaspoon salt and bring to a boil. Boil gently for about 20 minutes, skimming off scum as it forms. When scum no longer appears, turn heat down to maintain the merest simmer and cook for 1½ hours. Remove and discard carcass bones, leaving the rest in.

CHAUD-FROID (JELLIED WHITE SAUCE)

2 tablespoons butter
2 tablespoons flour
1 cup chicken stock from the poaching

1 envelope unflavored gelatin
2 tablespoons Amontillado Sherry
½ cup heavy cream
  Salt, if needed

Melt the butter in a small saucepan and stir in the flour. Remove from the heat and add the chicken stock, stirring until smooth. Bring to a boil over low heat and cook, stirring, for about 15 minutes, until sauce is thick and smooth.

Soften the gelatin with the Sherry in a 2-cup measure. Strain the sauce into it and stir until gelatin is dissolved. Add cream and mix well. Add a little salt if needed. Cool to room temperature and apply to galantine as described in recipe.

CLEAR ASPIC

3 cups cold stock from the poaching
  Salt to taste
2 envelopes unflavored gelatin
1 egg white, lightly beaten
1 eggshell, crushed
2 tablespoons Amontillado Sherry

Put the cold stock, salted to taste, in a large saucepan, and sprinkle the gelatin over it. Add the egg white and shell. Heat slowly, stirring constantly, until the mixture boils up. Remove from the heat and allow to stand, without stirring or moving, for 5 to 10 minutes. Strain the foamy mixture slowly through a sieve lined with several layers of dampened cheesecloth, without stirring or disturbing the residue. Discard residue. Stir the Sherry into the strained mixture, now a clear aspic.

If the stock is clear or only slightly cloudy, the egg white and shell can be omitted, as can the straining. In this case, just bring the stock and gelatin to a boil, stirring, pour into a bowl, and add the Sherry.

ASPIC WITH TOMATO

This is an aspic with a slight color to it, which can be used directly on the galantine (if you want to omit the Chaud-Froid) with or without decorations. If decorations are used, dip each element in the aspic and apply to the galantine. Chill to set, and then glaze with several thin coats of the aspic, chilling after each coat.

  3 cups cold stock from the poaching
  1 cup tomato juice
    Salt to taste
½ teaspoon sugar
  3 envelopes unflavored gelatin
  2 tablespoons Amontillado Sherry

Put the cold stock and tomato juice into a saucepan. Add salt, if needed, and sugar. Sprinkle gelatin on top. Bring to a boil, stirring constantly. Line a sieve with several layers of dampened cheesecloth and strain the mixture through it without pressing the residue through. Stir the Sherry into the strained mixture. Remove 1 cupful and cool to the consistency of egg white, by setting it in its container in a basin of ice and water and stirring. Use this to moisten the decorations, if used, and to coat the galantine. Return what is left to the rest of the aspic, heat to liquefy, and pour into a cake tin. Chill and serve chopped around the galantine.

Perhaps the easiest material for decoration is the green part of scallions. Sharply green against the ivory background of the Chaud-Froid, it makes a most elegant presentation. Choose scallions with plenty of fresh crisp green tops. Trim off the white part and any brown tips, and split the hollow green part open with scissors or a small sharp knife. Dip them in boiling water for a moment, and then in cold water, to make them limp and greener. Spread them out on a paper towel, inside surface up, and scrape away the slimy stuff with a dull knife. Spread them out on a cutting board, the other way up. They are now ready to be cut, with a sharp pointed knife, into the shapes you want. These can be long, tapering grass blade shapes, shorter leaf shapes, coming out of delicate stems, and tiny petals to top a stem.

A large carrot, scraped, boiled, and sliced very thinly lengthwise, provides material for orange petals, and the tip of a black olive makes a center.

Hard-cooked egg white makes white petals, and a tiny bit of the yolk, mashed and mixed with a little mayonnaise, can be placed in the center with the tip of a small knife. Pimiento and hard-cooked egg whites can both be made into tulip shapes at the tops of scallion stems, with scallion leaves at each side, perhaps with one realistically folded over.

Cima alla Genovese
Genoese Stuffed Veal

A sort of Italian galantine, this Genoese specialty depends for its glamour on the beauty of the slices rather than overall decoration, so it comes to the table sliced. The slices reveal hard-cooked egg, pistachios, spinach, and peas in the meat mixture. Calf's brain and sweetbread, either one or both, are usually part of the stuffing mixture. In this recipe it is the brain, but those who do not care for it may substitute ¼ pound ground pork. We have added a touch of nutmeg and lemon rind to the usual ingredients, which we feel is an improvement. We also like to serve a lemon wedge with it, and squeeze some juice on the slice.

Served as a first course, the Cima could be followed by another wonder from Genoa, Il Pesto, or Pesto alla Genovese, the great fresh basil sauce, on spaghetti. Or, still keeping the Italian theme, the main course could be Ossobuco (braised veal shanks) with Risotto.* Any favorite Italian dish would be good after the Cima: lasagne, stuffed manicotti, spaghetti with clam sauce, or just Spaghetti with Garlic Sauce,* followed by a big tossed salad, plenty of Italian bread, and fresh fruit.

Served as the focus of a buffet, the Cima could share the table with
an abundance of other good things to eat, easily prepared or found
in jars or cans or in stores specializing in Italian foods. A few suggestions: whole pimientos; Hot Potato Salad;* wedges of canta-
loupe wrapped in thin slices of prosciutto; black olives and strips
of fennel, romaine, celery, and scallions with their tops; marinated
mushrooms; marinated artichoke hearts; a tray of Italian cheeses;
and plenty of Italian bread.

Fruity, rounded reds like a Barolo suit this loaf, as do big Rhônes
like Hermitage or Côte Rôtie, the Côte de Beaune estate-bottlings,
or a less expensive California Pinot Noir or Gamay.

Serve the same day as the cooking, if there is time enough for thorough chilling. It is even better the following day or up to a week
later. Keep well wrapped and refrigerated.

Breast of veal (4½–5 pounds), boned, bones reserved

½ pound calf's brain (*or* ¼ pound ground pork)
  Salt
1 tablespoon vinegar
2 tablespoons butter
1 small onion, chopped

¼ pound ground veal
¼ pound fresh pork fat, from the loin or fresh ham in ¼-inch dice
1 ten-ounce package frozen chopped spinach, defrosted and squeezed dry
2 slices firm white home-style bread, crusts removed
¼ cup milk
⅓ cup grated Parmesan cheese

1 egg
2 teaspoons salt
¼ teaspoon freshly ground black pepper
½ teaspoon marjoram
  Good pinch of nutmeg
1 clove garlic, minced
  Grated rind of ½ lemon

1 cup defrosted frozen peas
½ cup shelled pistachio nuts
3 hard-cooked eggs

  Veal bones
1 onion, coarsely chopped
2 cloves garlic
1 carrot, scraped

2 parsley sprigs
1 bay leaf
4 cans ready-to-use chicken broth (13¾-ounce size)

Salt and pepper to taste

Parsley sprigs to garnish

Ask the butcher to bone the veal and cut a pocket in it. Save the bones for stock.

To prepare the calf's brain, soak it for 2 hours. Drain, rinse, and put into a saucepan with cold salted water. (Use 1 teaspoon per quart of water.) Bring to a boil. Drain again and put back in the pan with fresh salted water and 1 tablespoon vinegar. Bring to a boil, turn the heat down, and simmer until tender, about 15 minutes. Remove from the water and trim off as much skin and membrane as possible without tearing meat. Chop finely.

In a small skillet, heat the butter and slowly cook the onions and brain until the onions are soft. Put the mixture into a large mixing bowl. If pork is used instead of brain, put it into the mixing bowl uncooked.

Put the veal, pork fat, and spinach into the bowl. Moisten the bread with the milk and crumble it into the bowl. Sprinkle the Parmesan cheese on top.

In a small bowl, lightly beat the egg and mix in the seasonings, garlic, and lemon rind. Add to the contents of the large mixing bowl and mix with the hands or beat with a wooden spoon until well mixed and light.

Carefully stir in the peas and nuts. Push half the mixture into the pocket of the veal, spreading it on the bottom. Put the hard-cooked eggs in, in a row lengthwise, end to end. Spoon in the rest of the meat mixture, covering the eggs completely. Sew up the opening with strong white thread.

Put the stuffed veal into a deep heavy casserole or kettle that will allow for liquid to cover it, add the stock ingredients, and water to cover. Taste and add salt if needed, and pepper. Bring to a boil, turn down the heat, and cook at the merest simmer for 1½ hours or until tender. Cook uncovered for the first hour, covered for the rest of the time. Allow the Cima to cool in the stock. When it is cool, refrigerate for several hours or overnight. Remove thread and serve in quarter-inch slices, garnished with parsley. It will serve 6 to 8, or 8 to 10 if it is served as a first course or in a buffet. The stock can be strained and frozen for other uses.

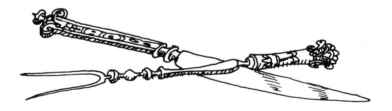

PÂTÉS IN PASTRY

Pâté en Croûte
Veal, Pork, and Ham Loaf in Pastry

This elegant little loaf is very easy to make. It consists of equal parts of veal, pork, pork fat, and ham, the ham in marinated strips embedded in the ground meat to make a pattern in the slices. If truffles were not so ridiculously expensive this would be a good place to use them; we have listed them as an optional ingredient. Resplendent in its pastry case, the pâté makes a fine first course and needs only salad, crusty bread, a cheese tray, and fruit to serve as a main-course luncheon or supper dish. You can also use it for a picnic; pack stemmed wine glasses to take along.

Some people like fine Rhine wines or Extra-Sec Champagne with pâtés in pastry, but a soft, matured red from Burgundy's Côte de Beaune, or from Graves or the Haut-Médoc in Bordeaux, can be very satisfying too.

The pâté can be served the day it is made if there is enough time for the chilling. It keeps up to a week, well covered and refrigerated. Remove it from the refrigerator about an hour before serving.

For 5-cup loaf pan (8½″ x 4½″ x 2½″)

½ pound cooked ham ⅜ inch thick, in ⅜-inch strips
1 truffle in ¼-inch julienne with juice (optional)
2–3 tablespoons Madeira
    Pinch each of pepper, thyme, allspice

1¼ teaspoons salt *or* 1 teaspoon if ham is very salty
½ teaspoon freshly ground black pepper
2 eggs
2 tablespoons Cognac
½ pound ground veal
½ pound ground lean pork
½ pound pork fat (from loin or fresh ham), coarsely chopped

1 recipe for pastry* (leftover pastry can be frozen)
1 egg beaten with 1 tablespoon milk for glaze

1 can ready-to-use chicken broth (13¾-ounce size)
1 envelope unflavored gelatin
2 tablespoons Cognac

    Parsley or watercress to garnish

Put the ham strips and truffle (if used) in a small bowl with the Madeira, pepper, thyme, and allspice and allow to marinate for 2 hours, stirring occasionally. The ham should be from a leftover baked ham or sliced from a delicatessen boiled or baked ham or cut from a ham steak, fully cooked and trimmed of fat and bone.

Put the salt, pepper, eggs, and Cognac in the blender and give them a short whirl. Mix the veal, pork, and pork fat together and add, a little at a time, to the blender, whirling after each addition until all has been added, and stopping to scrape down the sides occasionally. Remove to a bowl.

Butter a 5-cup loaf pan lightly. Cut a strip of heavy foil long enough to cover the bottom and the two long sides of the pan and to allow an overhang of 2 to 3 inches on each side. Butter this strip, place in the pan, and lightly flour foil and the short ends of the pan. The foil makes a kind of sling for the loaf, with which to lift it from the pan when cooked.

Roll out the pastry ⅛ to ¼ inch thick. Cut a piece of pastry the same size as the foil, roll it over the rolling pin, and unroll into the pan. Trim it to go just over the edges. Press the pastry carefully into the pan without stretching it and without making any holes. Make the rest of the pastry into a ball and roll out again. Cut two pieces for the ends of the pan and seal them to the other pastry with egg glaze. Press seams with a small floured wad of pastry to avoid making holes with the nails.

Remove the ham strips (and truffle strips) from the marinade and mix the juices with the meat mixture. Pack a third of the meat mixture into the pastry-lined pan, lay half of the marinated strips along the meat, and cover with another layer of meat. Put the rest of the marinated strips on top and gently mound the rest of the meat mixture on top. Turn the edges of the pastry over the loaf and paint with egg glaze. Roll out the rest of the pastry for the top, pressing and sealing well. Crimp with fingers or a fork. Make a 1½-inch hole in the center of the loaf and put in a cone made of foil, or a small metal funnel, for the fat to come up into, and through which you will pour aspic when the loaf is cold. Cut out a few little circles or leaf shapes from scraps of pastry and stick them on the pastry top with egg glaze, and paint the whole top, decorations and all, with glaze, using a soft brush or fingers. Bake in preheated 350° oven for 1¼ to 1½ hours, or until the fat coming up into the funnel is clear, not pinkish or cloudy. If pastry starts to brown too quickly, cover lightly with two pieces of foil, one for each side of the funnel. The pastry can be brushed with glaze a couple of times during cooking.

Remove from the oven and allow to cool in the pan. When cool, refrigerate. Remove and clear the funnel. Chill well.

To make aspic, cook chicken broth over high heat for about 5 minutes to reduce it to 1½ cups. Moisten the gelatin with the Cognac and add to the broth, stirring until dissolved. Cool by setting pan in ice water and stirring until the aspic is beginning to set but is still runny. Replace the funnel in the cold loaf and carefully pour the aspic into it, tipping the loaf to let the aspic find the spaces where the loaf has shrunk from the pastry. Keep pouring in until it will not take any more. Wait for ten minutes and add more aspic. Repeat until about half the aspic has been used. Chill the loaf again for aspic to set, and chill leftover aspic to be served chopped around the loaf.

To remove from the pan, hold the pan in 2 inches of hot water for a moment, run a knife or spatula between the pastry and pan at the small ends, and, grasping the foil overhangs at each side, lift the loaf from the pan. Slide off the foil onto a serving board or platter. Decorate with a little parsley or watercress and chopped aspic and serve sliced, after presenting it intact to be admired. Yields about 14 half-inch slices.

Pâté Pantin
Pork and Veal Pâté in Pastry

A Pantin pâté can be a cylindrical or a crescent-shaped loaf in pastry. This one is more or less oval, the well-seasoned meat mixture simply wrapped in pastry and baked on a cookie sheet. Although it uses only a pound of meat, it will serve 4 to 6 as a first course. Slightly smaller than the preceding Pâté en Croûte, it can be served in the same ways and with the same wines, as a first course, a main course for a little luncheon or supper, a buffet item, or for a splendid picnic.

The pâté can be served the day it is made, with enough time allowed for chilling. It is good up to a week later, kept well covered and refrigerated. Remove from the refrigerator about an hour before serving.

Baked on a cookie sheet

½ pound ground lean pork
¼ pound pork fat (from loin or fresh ham)
¼ pound ground veal

1 egg
1 teaspoon salt
¼ teaspoon freshly ground black pepper
⅛ teaspoon rosemary, finely crumbled
¼ teaspoon summer savory
¼ bay leaf, finely crumbled
¼ cup Port

1 recipe for pastry* (leftover pastry can be frozen)
1 egg beaten with 1 tablespoon milk for glaze

Aspic as for Pâté en Croûte (page 118)

Put pork, finely chopped pork fat, and veal in a large mixing bowl.

In a small bowl, lightly beat the egg, add the seasonings and Port, and mix well. Add to the meats and mix thoroughly.

Roll out the pastry to a rectangle ⅛ to ¼ inch thick. Make the meat mixture into a roll about 3 inches in diameter. Set it on the pastry and trim the pastry to about 3 inches beyond the loaf at the sides and about 4 inches at each end. Bring the pastry up to cover the sides and ends of the loaf. Trim the corners and seal with egg glaze. Roll out remaining pastry to ⅛-inch thickness to make a top for the loaf that will overlap the edges already on by ½ inch or more, sealing them together with egg glaze. Press the edges together with the tines of a fork or the dull side of a knife, to make a pattern and to make sure they are well sealed. Cut a hole ½ inch in diameter in the center of the loaf. Cut leaf shapes, circles, strips, or crescents out of the scraps of pastry for decoration. Stick them on the loaf with egg glaze, and paint the entire loaf liberally with the glaze, using the fingers or a soft brush.

Insert a small metal funnel, or one made of foil, into the hole in the loaf, for juices to bubble up into and for the addition of aspic later. Set the loaf on a buttered and lightly floured cookie sheet, and place in a preheated 375° oven. Immediately turn oven down to 350° and bake for 60 to 70 minutes, or until pastry is beautifully brown and juices in the funnel are clear, not pink or cloudy. If pastry starts to brown too quickly, cover with 2 pieces of foil, one on each side of the funnel.

Cool to room temperature and then refrigerate. Remove and clear the funnel. When the loaf is thoroughly chilled, after several hours or overnight, make the aspic. Cool the aspic in a basin of ice and water, stirring constantly, until it is the consistency of egg whites. Pour the aspic into the loaf through the funnel, a little at a time, tipping the loaf to allow the aspic to get to the ends and sides. The aspic fills the spaces left by the shrinkage of the loaf during cooking. When no more aspic will go in, refrigerate the loaf for another couple of hours to set. (Leftover aspic can be chilled, chopped, and served around the loaf.) Remove from the refrigerator an hour before serving. Cut into slices. Serves 4 to 6 for a first course.

Raised Pork Pie

Those with England, Scotland, or Canada in their background may remember this cold pork loaf in pastry as a popular cold supper item, along with ham or tongue and homemade pickles, with home-preserved fruit and a bit of cake for dessert. It always looked wonderful but was usually bland in taste, and the pastry was almost invariably terrible. This recipe has a well-seasoned filling and uses the rich and delicate butter and lard pastry given in the back of this book, which we find infinitely more edible.

The name Raised Pork Pie derives from the way the pastry used to be made. The method was to boil water and lard together and add the mixture to salted flour, mixing and kneading until the dough was the consistency of modeling clay. It was then shaped into an oval or a round container for the meat, the sides being "raised" around an oval wooden mold or a round glass jar. The mold or jar removed, the shell was filled and topped with a pastry lid, pinned or tied in a wrapping of greased paper, and baked. This version is baked in a loaf pan. We have suggested a long 8-cup pan because it makes smaller slices, but the regular 9-by-5-by-3-inch pan can be used perfectly well, with slightly longer cooking because it is deeper.

The loaf makes a fine first course or a hearty luncheon or supper dish, with a salad, cheese, and fruit. Preceded by a soup and served with a hot vegetable or two, it can serve as a main course. Either red or white wines, inexpensive ones like Beaujolais or Liebfraumilch, go well, and so do beer, ale, or cider.

The loaf can be served the day it is made, if started early enough for chilling, and it improves with keeping up to a week, well wrapped and refrigerated. Remove from refrigerator about an hour before serving.

For long 8-cup loaf pan (13" x 4½" x 2½")

   1 recipe for pastry*

  ¼ pound fresh pork fat, in ½-inch cubes (from the loin or fresh ham)

1½ pounds lean pork, in ½-inch cubes

   1 teaspoon salt

  ½ teaspoon freshly ground black pepper

   1 pound ground pork shoulder

   4 slices lean bacon, diced

  ¼ cup finely chopped fresh parsley

   1 teaspoon grated lemon rind

  ⅓ cup Cognac

   1 tablespoon lemon juice

  ¼ teaspoon salt

  ¼ teaspoon sage, crumbled

  ½ teaspoon marjoram

  ½ teaspoon savory, crumbled

  ⅛ teaspoon mace

   1 egg lightly beaten with 1 tablespoon milk for glaze

½–¾ pound thinly sliced Canadian bacon
     Pickled walnuts, split lengthwise (optional)

   1 can ready-to-use chicken broth (13¾-ounce size)

   1 envelope unflavored gelatin

   2 tablespoons Port

   1 tablespoon lemon juice

Make the pastry and refrigerate for at least ½ hour.

In a heavy skillet, render the pork fat just enough to oil the pan slightly. Add the diced pork and cook, stirring, until the pork has lost its pink color and is barely beginning to brown. Sprinkle with the salt and pepper and remove with a slotted spoon to a large mixing bowl. Allow to cool.

Add the ground pork, diced bacon, parsley, and lemon rind to the mixing bowl and mix lightly.

In a small bowl, combine the Cognac, lemon juice, salt, sage, marjoram, savory, and mace. Add to the meat mixture and mix well.

Butter a long 8-cup loaf pan. To make a kind of sling for the loaf so it can be lifted out of the pan when it is cooked, cut a piece of heavy foil to cover the bottom and both long sides of the pan, with a 3-inch overhang on each side. Fit the foil into the pan and butter it. Shake a little flour around the pan to lightly coat foil and small ends of the pan. Discard excess.

Reserve one-fourth of the pastry for the top of the loaf. Roll out the other three-fourths to a thickness of 1/8 to 1/4 inch, and cut a piece roughly the same size as the foil. Drape it over the rolling pin and unroll it into the pan to cover the foil, being careful not to stretch it or make any holes. Make pieces of pastry to fit the ends of the pan, allowing for 1/2-inch overlap. Fit the end pieces into the pan, sealing the overlap with egg glaze. Roll the pin over the rim to trim off excess pastry.

Line the bottom and all four sides of the pastry with the Canadian bacon. Gently pack half the meat into the pan, pressing and patting into corners. Place pickled walnuts, if used, in a line down the middle. Add the rest of the meat, doming it slightly. Fold the edges of the pastry over the edges of the loaf, trimming corners to avoid excess thickness.

To make the top, roll out the reserved quarter of the pastry to ⅛- to ¼-inch thickness and trim to 6½ by 15 inches. Paint the edges of the pastry in the pan with the egg glaze, drape the pastry over the rolling pin, and unroll it over the loaf, pressing the edges to seal. Trim off excess. Cut a hole ½ inch in diameter in the center of the loaf. Roll out pastry scraps a little thinner than the rest, and cut out strips, leaf shapes, circles, or crescents, paint them on the bottom with egg glaze, and stick them on for decoration. Crimp the edges with the tines of a fork or the dull side of a knife, and paint the entire top with glaze.

Set a small metal funnel, or one made of foil, into the hole in the top, to accommodate juices that bubble up during cooking. Set in the middle of a preheated 375° oven. Turn oven down to 350° immediately and cook for 1¼ to 1½ hours, or until loaf is beautifully brown and the juices that can be seen in the funnel are clear, not pink or opaque. Remove from the oven and allow to stand for 2 hours.

To make aspic, cook chicken broth over high heat for about 5 minutes to reduce it to 1½ cups. Moisten the gelatin with the Port and lemon juice and add to the broth, stirring until dissolved. Set the container of aspic in a basin of ice and water and cool, stirring, until it is the consistency of egg whites.

Pour the aspic into the loaf through the funnel, a little at a time, waiting for each addition to be absorbed before adding more. This operation can be done over the period of an hour or so while you are doing other things. The loaf has to cool to room temperature before refrigerating anyway. Try to get in about half the aspic. When the loaf has come to room temperature, refrigerate for 4 hours or overnight. When the loaf has been thoroughly chilled, bring the remaining aspic back to egg-white consistency and try to get more into the loaf through the cleaned funnel, tipping the pan from end to end each time to spread aspic throughout. This rather tiresome step is to fill with aspic the spaces left by the shrinkage of the loaf during cooking. Leftover aspic can be chilled and served chopped with the loaf. Chill the loaf another 2 hours or longer, and take it out of the refrigerator an hour before serving.

To unmold, run a knife between loaf and pan at the small ends, immerse pan in a few inches of hot water for a moment or two, and carefully lift out, using the foil overhangs as handles. Slide off the foil onto a platter or board and serve in half-inch slices. You will have about 15 half-inch slices if you use the 9-by-5-by-3-inch pan or about 22 half-inch slices from the longer pan.

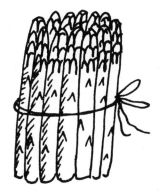

JELLIED LOAVES AND MOUSSES

Sülze
Jellied Veal and Pork Loaf

Sülze, pronounced *zilts-eh*, belongs to the family of jellied loaves that includes the Jewish Petcha, made of veal only, also called calf's-foot jelly, and the English head cheese, made of the meat from the pig's head. Although the recipe may look formidable at first glance, it is really a simple matter of simmering bones and meat together and making a loaf of the meat and the reduced stock. Theoretically, they are supposed to produce their own gelatin, which they do, but not enough for the firmness required for easy slicing, so they usually have added gelatin. The trick is the seasoning, which varies but in most cases includes some vinegar for piquancy. This version, with its main seasoning of pickling spice, a touch of vinegar, and Tabasco sauce, is one you will want to have around for a high-protein nonfat snack as well as for its other uses.

Good for first course, luncheon, or picnic, the loaf's distinctive taste is enhanced by a rosé—from Provence, Tavel, or Anjou—or a crisp white from the Loire, like Sancerre or Pouilly-Fumé, or an Alsatian white like Traminer or Sylvaner.

Sülze can be served the day it is made if there is time for several hours of chilling. It keeps for a week, well wrapped and refrigerated.

For 5-cup loaf pan (8½" x 4½" x 2½")

2½–3 pounds veal shank or shoulder, bones and meat
   1 pound veal knuckle, split
   2 pounds fresh pork hocks
   1 teaspoon salt
    Boiling water to cover

   1 tablespoon pickling spice
 10 peppercorns
   4 celery stalks
   4 large parsley sprigs, with stems

   1 envelope powdered beef bouillon *or* 1 beef bouillon cube
  ½ teaspoon salt or more, to taste
  ¼ teaspoon freshly ground black pepper
    Few drops Tabasco sauce, more to taste
   1 teaspoon wine vinegar

1½ envelopes unflavored gelatin
   2 tablespoons dry white wine *or* cooled stock

    Hard-cooked egg slices, pimiento-stuffed olive slices,
    cooked thin carrot rounds, *or* black olive slices to decorate

    Parsley sprigs or watercress to garnish

Place bones, meat, and salt in a large pot and cover with boiling water. Bring back to a gentle boil, and remove scum as it forms.

When scum stops forming, add the pickling spice, peppercorns, celery, and parsley. Adjust heat to maintain an even simmer.

After 1½ hours of cooking, start testing the meat. It is done when it is tender and falling off the bones. As pieces are done, remove them with tongs to a colander set over a bowl. Pull the bones free of the meat and put the bones back in the pot, to cook another 1½ to 2 hours. When the meat has cooled enough to handle, remove and reserve the pork hock skin, and trim fat and hard gristle from the meat. Don't discard any gelatinous matter as long as it is tender. Chop the meat into ¼-inch dice, place in a bowl that will just accommodate it, moisten with some stock (there may be enough in the bowl under the colander), and cover with scraps and skin to keep it from drying out.

When the stock has cooked a total of 3 to 3½ hours from the end of the scum formation (1½ to 2 hours after the meat has been removed), take out the bones and strain the stock through a strainer lined with several layers of dampened cheesecloth. Skim fat from the top of the stock. (This process may be facilitated by putting the bowl of stock in a basin of ice and water, or in the freezer briefly, to cool it so the fat will harden and be easy to remove.) Measure the stock: if it is more than 3½ to 4 cups, cook it down to that amount; if it is less, add water to bring it up to that amount.

Put the stock into a saucepan and add the bouillon, salt, pepper, Tabasco, and vinegar. Taste and adjust seasoning. (When the stock has jelled, some flavor will be masked, so give it a good strong taste.) Bring to a boil.

Moisten the gelatin with wine or stock and add it to the hot broth, stirring until the gelatin is dissolved.

Pour ¼ inch of stock mixture, now aspic, into a small 5-cup loaf pan and set it in the basin of ice and water, or in the freezer for a few minutes, until it sets. Make a pattern of your chosen garnish on the set gelatin, spoon a little bit of aspic over the decorations, and allow it to set.

Remove and discard the skin and scraps covering the chopped meats, drain off the liquid, and pack the meat loosely into the loaf pan on top of the decorations, being careful not to disturb the design. When aspic is cool but not yet jelling, pour over the meat, filling the pan to within ½ inch of the top. (You may save and refrigerate any leftover aspic, when it has cooled to room temperature, for other uses.) When the loaf is cool, refrigerate until set— 8 hours or overnight.

To unmold, run a knife around the edge of the loaf and immerse the pan in an inch or so of hot water for a few moments. Invert onto a platter and surround with parsley or watercress. The decorations are now on top. Serve in half-inch slices with a light wine vinegar, Vinaigrette Dressing* with plenty of minced shallots or scallions in it, or Dijon mustard. Yields 14 or 15 half-inch slices.

Jellied Lamb Loaf, Chinese Style

Soy sauce, Sherry, fresh ginger, and scallions give this loaf its distinctly Chinese taste, and the soy sauce makes it a beautiful dark brown. It can be made of the kind of lamb that comes in a package containing an assortment of pieces, some chops, some pieces of good stewing meat, and a few pieces that are more bone than meat.

Useful for an hors-d'oeuvre, first course, luncheon, buffet, or picnic, or, like Sülze, a low-calorie, high-protein snack any time, this subtle, interesting loaf goes with a great variety of drinkables. Tea or beer is fine with it, but wine lovers might like to experiment with a whole range of possibilities. Dry Fino or Manzanilla Sherry, well chilled, is excellent with it, but a light German white—a Rheingau or Moselle from the Riesling grape—may be even better. Most unusual of all might be a Gewürztraminer or Tokay d'Alsace. Even rosés and light reds taste good—a Tavel or Grenache Rosé, or a Graves or St. Émilion from Bordeaux.

The loaf can be served the day it is made if there is time for several hours of chilling. It keeps up to a week, well wrapped and refrigerated.

For 5-cup pan (8½" x 4½" x 2½") or mold

3–3½   pounds lamb shoulder, stew meat, and chops, with bones
    1   can chicken broth (13¾-ounce size)
    3   cups water to cover
    3   slices fresh ginger

4 scallions, with green tops
 ½ cup soy sauce
   2 tablespoons Amontillado Sherry
   1 tablespoon sugar

1½ envelopes unflavored gelatin
   3 tablespoons Amontillado Sherry

   Scallion pieces to garnish

Trim off and discard large pieces of fat from the lamb and place it in a heavy, lidded pot (preferably enameled ironware) with the chicken broth, water, ginger, scallions, soy sauce, Sherry, and sugar. Bring to a gentle boil, and skim off scum as long as it appears, about 10 minutes. Lower the heat and simmer, partially covered, for 1½ to 2 hours, or until all the meat is very tender. Take out small pieces as they are done and keep them moist with a little stock. When all the meat is done, set it aside with the smaller pieces and keep moist and covered. Discard the bones. Strain the stock through a strainer lined with several layers of dampened cheesecloth, and measure it. There should be about 4 cups. Rinse the pot and put the stock back in. Boil over high heat to reduce to 2 cups. If it has boiled away to less than 2 cups, add water to make 2 cups. Skim off the fat.

In a 2-cup measure, moisten the gelatin with the Sherry. Bring the degreased stock to a boil and add to the gelatin, stirring to dissolve completely.

Remove remaining bits of fat from the lamb and pack the meat into a small (5-cup) loaf pan. Pour the stock over it, cool to room temperature, and refrigerate for about 6 hours or overnight.

Jellied Lamb Loaf, Chinese Style / 133

To unmold, run a knife around the edge of the loaf, immerse the pan in a few inches of hot water for a moment or two, and invert onto a cold platter. Garnish with 3-inch pieces of scallion cut into fine horizontal strips, and serve some of the onion with each slice. Yields 15 half-inch slices.

Mousse de Jambon
Ham Mousse

This little mousse is so full of flavor it will serve 6 to 8 people as a first course. The sight of a portion, pink and light on a lettuce leaf, with parsley or watercress, wedges of hard-cooked eggs, and toast triangles, makes the transition from cocktails to wine an easy one— it so obviously calls for a fresh cool white wine.

The ham should be leftovers from a baked ham, or sliced from a good delicatessen boiled or baked ham, or a piece cut from a fully cooked ham steak, trimmed of fat and bone. One tightly packed cup of chopped ham is about ½ pound of ham.

The most simple of meals can follow the mousse—slices from a cold roast, with asparagus or artichokes in French* or Vinaigrette Dressing,* and potato salad, for a cold meal; a *fines herbes* omelette with spinach, or a spinach soufflé, with sliced tomatoes for a hot one. Served as a main course for 4 to 6, the mousse could be accompanied by a watercress and endive salad (or a leafy one with lots of cucumber for crispness), French or Italian bread, and cheese and fruit.

White wine, such as a Sancerre or Muscadet from the Loire or a

California Chardonnay, would be good with the mousse and the suggested main courses to follow, and a rosé would not be out of place.

The mousse can be made the day it is to be served, if several hours are allowed for chilling. It keeps for two or three days, well wrapped and refrigerated.

For 4-cup mold

2 tablespoons minced shallots *or* the white part of scallions
1 tablespoon butter
1 cup canned chicken broth

1 envelope unflavored gelatin
2 tablespoons dry white wine *or* dry Vermouth
1 cup chopped lean cooked ham, tightly packed

1 tablespoon finely chopped pimiento
¼ cup finely chopped celery
¼ cup finely chopped green pepper
1 teaspoon Dijon mustard
2 tablespoons tomato paste
1 tablespoon Madeira or Cognac
  Salt and freshly ground black pepper

⅓ cup heavy cream

  Parsley sprigs or watercress to garnish
  Hard-cooked eggs, radishes, or cherry tomatoes to decorate

In a small skillet or saucepan, slowly cook the shallots or scallions in butter until they are soft but not brown. Add the chicken broth and bring to a simmer. Pour into the blender.

Add the gelatin, softened in the wine, to the blender, and a little bit of the ham. Whirl briefly, add more ham, and whirl again. Add the rest of the ham and blend until just smooth.

Pour the blended mixture into a mixing bowl and stir in the pimiento, celery, green pepper, mustard, tomato paste, and liquor. Season with salt and pepper to taste; don't make it too bland because there is cream to be added. The amount of salt depends on how salty your ham and broth are. Add more liquor if desired. Refrigerate the mixture, stirring occasionally, until it is beginning to set.

Whip the cream and fold it into the mixture. Pour into a lightly buttered mold and bang the pan on the table to get rid of air holes. Refrigerate several hours until it is set.

To unmold, run a knife around the edge, hold the pan briefly in an inch or so of hot water, and invert onto a platter or plate. Serve decorated with parsley or watercress and hard-cooked egg wedges, and perhaps some radishes or cherry tomatoes for more color. Serves 6 to 8 as a first course, 4 to 6 for a main-course luncheon dish.

This is a good way to use leftover roast chicken or turkey. However, if you want to start from scratch, here is a recipe for cooking chicken breasts:

2 cans ready-to-use chicken broth (13¾-ounce size)
4 slices carrot
3 slices onion
1 sprig parsley
  Large pinch each of pepper and thyme
3 chicken breast halves, skinned, boned, and trimmed of fat

Simmer chicken broth with vegetables and spices for 20 minutes. Poach breasts in the simmering stock for 6 to 8 minutes or until just done. Drain, discard vegetables, reserve 1 cup of the stock, and cool and chop breasts.

Proceed with the recipe for Ham Mousse, adjusted in the following ways:

1. Use 1½ cups chopped cooked chicken or turkey, either all breast or breast and dark meat, instead of the ham.
2. Omit the mustard and tomato paste.
3. Increase the Madeira to 2 tablespoons.
4. Use the richer stock saved from poaching the chicken breasts. Or, if leftover meat is used, make a richer broth by bringing the can of chicken broth to a boil with 3 slices of carrot, 2 slices of onion, a sprig of parsley, and a pinch each of pepper and thyme; simmering for 20 to 30 minutes, or until reduced to 1 cup; and then straining.

Second Variation: Crabmeat Mousse

Follow the recipe for Ham Mousse adjusted in the following ways:

1. Use 1 seven-ounce can of crabmeat, and its juice, instead of the ham. Pick over the crabmeat carefully to remove any pieces of shell.
2. Omit pimiento, green pepper, mustard, and tomato paste.
3. Add ¼ cup finely chopped fresh parsley.
4. Use the Madeira, or Amontillado Sherry, rather than the Cognac, and add 2 tablespoons lemon juice.

Salmon Loaf

Light and refreshing for summer or any time of the year, this loaf can serve as a first course or part of a buffet, as well as a main-course luncheon or supper dish. On a lettuce leaf, with mayonnaise, it could precede a roast, chops, steak, or stew. For a buffet, garnished with thin slices of lemon, drained Sweet-Sour Cucumbers,* or hard-cooked eggs, it could share the table with a pâté or terrine and the good things that accompany it, taking the place of shrimp or smoked salmon. By itself, all it needs is a potato salad, hard-cooked eggs, and sliced tomatoes. Practically any dry white wine complements this loaf, particularly those from the Rhine. A Tavel or Grenache Rosé would also be good.

For 4-cup mold or 5-cup loaf pan, not tin-lined

1 one-pound can salmon

1 medium cucumber

¼ cup lemon juice
½ teaspoon salt

2 envelopes unflavored gelatin
3 tablespoons Amontillado Sherry mixed with 3
  tablespoons water

1½ ounces cream cheese
½ cup sour cream
1 cup cottage cheese
½ cup finely chopped scallions with green tops
1 cup finely chopped celery
¼ cup finely chopped fresh parsley
2 tablespoons finely chopped green pepper
1 tablespoon capers, minced
1 teaspoon chopped fresh dill *or* ¼ teaspoon dried dill
½ teaspoon freshly ground black pepper
½ teaspoon salt, or more to taste

Additional parsley (or watercress) to garnish

Drain the salmon, remove black skin, and mash or discard bones. Discard juice and flake the salmon. Set aside.

Peel and coarsely chop the cucumber, and purée it in the blender, seeds and all, until smooth. In a small saucepan, combine 1 cup of the purée, the lemon juice, and the salt. Bring just to a boil.

In a 2-cup measure, moisten the gelatin with the Sherry and water, and add the hot cucumber-lemon mixture, stirring to dissolve the gelatin completely. Set aside to cool.

Mash the cream cheese with the sour cream and combine with the scallions, celery, parsley, green pepper, capers, dill, pepper, and salt. Fold in the salmon and the cooled but not setting gelatin mixture. Check for salt, adding more if necessary, pour into a 4-cup mold or 5-cup loaf pan, and chill for 6 hours or overnight.

To unmold, run a knife around the edge of the loaf, hold the pan in an inch or so of hot water for a moment, and invert onto a cold platter. Sprinkle with chopped parsley and surround with watercress or parsley sprigs. Serves 4 to 6.

Hot Loaves

PASTRY-COVERED LOAVES

Beef Loaf in Pastry

One pound of ground beef makes this hearty pastry-covered loaf which will serve 4 to 6, depending on the way it is served. With just a salad, followed by a cheese course and dessert, it could serve 4. Preceded by a soup and accompanied by two vegetables, it could be enough for 6. The vegetables could be any of the following combinations: mashed yellow turnip and green peas; parsleyed potatoes and asparagus; Scalloped Potatoes* and grilled tomatoes; Spaghetti with Garlic Sauce* and zucchini. Any of the hot sauces given in the back of the book would be good to serve along with the loaf.

Beer would be good to drink or, for wine, a California Mountain Red or a rosé.

Baked on an edged cookie sheet

> 1 pound ground beef chuck
> 1 medium onion, chopped
> 1 teaspoon salt
> ½ teaspoon freshly ground black pepper
> 3–4 slices firm white home-style bread, crusts removed
> ¼ cup dry red wine
> ⅔ cup beef broth (ready-to-use canned or made with a bouillon cube—1 cube to 1 cup water)
>
> 1 recipe for pastry*
> 1 egg beaten with 1 tablespoon milk for glaze
>
> Parsley or watercress to garnish

Put the beef, onion, salt, and pepper in a large mixing bowl. Coarsely crumble, or tear into small pieces, the bread, to make 1½ cups. Add to the seasoned meat. Add the wine and broth and mix thoroughly; the mixture will be quite moist. Cover and refrigerate for 8 hours or overnight. When ready to use, mix again.

Roll out pastry to a rectangle roughly 15 by 10 inches and ⅛ to ¼ inch thick. Trim the edges, and lay the meat down the center the long way, in a roll about 2½ inches in diameter, to within 2 inches of each end. Bring one long side of the pastry up over the meat, brush the edge generously with the egg glaze, and bring up the other side to cover, pressing gently to seal. Pinch the ends together, using some of the egg glaze to seal. Make 3 holes, evenly spaced down the middle of the pastry, ½ inch in diameter. Cover the join on top of the roll, between the holes, with little rounds or leaf shapes of pastry made out of rolled-out scraps. Fasten them on with egg glaze, and paint the entire loaf, decorations and all, with the glaze. Don't fuss with the decorations, except to be sure there are no holes in the pastry other than the ones you have made. No matter how roughly it is done, the roll will look beautiful when it comes out of the oven.

Place the roll on a floured cookie sheet and bake in a preheated 400° oven, in the lower third of the oven, for 20 minutes. Turn oven to 375° and cook the roll in the middle or upper third of the oven for another 20 to 25 minutes, or until pastry is nicely browned. If for some reason pastry starts to get too brown in the first 20 minutes, cover lightly with foil. Remove from the oven and allow to stand for 15 minutes before transferring to a warm platter. Surround with parsley or watercress and serve in 1-inch slices. Serves 4 to 6.

English Pasties

These meat-filled pastry cylinders are also called Cornish Pasties, pronounced *pass-teez*. They are usually made as turnovers, but at the Vassels' very successful bakery in Toronto, Canada, from which this recipe comes, this popular item was even more popular when it was made in cylinder form. The bakery no longer exists, unfortunately, but we are happy to be able to perpetuate one of the recipes, even though, for lack of space, we are not able to give the particular pastry recipe which was so kindly offered. The good beefy taste should please anyone, even children. The ground beef is mixed with onions, carrots, and potatoes, not a great deal but enough to add flavor and texture. The meat and vegetable mixture does have to stand overnight, though, for the moisture to be absorbed and the flavor of the simple seasonings to permeate the meat, one of the Vassels' secrets. Once made, the finished rolls can be frozen either cooked or uncooked. Cooked pasties must be thoroughly cooled before freezing. After freezing, allow them to come to room temperature before reheating in a preheated 400° oven for about 10 minutes. Uncooked pasties, once defrosted, can be cooked as in the recipe.

The pasties make a good hot item for a buffet or to have with cocktails, either 4 inches long, as given here, or cut into 2-inch lengths before baking. Served as a main course for luncheon or supper, they need to be accompanied by something rather moist, like cole slaw or sliced tomatoes. For a more substantial meal, Hot Potato Salad* or home-fried potatoes with scallions and chopped parsley in them could be added, or Potatoes, Onions, or Celery in Cream Sauce,* made ahead and kept warm in a chafing dish. Any of the hot sauces given in the back of the book would be good to serve along with the pasties. Stewed fruit or sherbet, with cake or cookies, would make a nice simple dessert.

Beer, particularly English Ale or Stout, would go well with the pasties, or any dry wine, red or white, but there is nothing wrong with a good cup of tea.

Baked on an edged cookie sheet or jelly-roll pan

  1 recipe for pastry*
  1 egg lightly beaten with 1 tablespoon milk for glaze

  2 pounds lean ground beef
  2 medium onions, finely chopped

2 medium carrots, finely chopped
2 medium potatoes, chopped a little more coarsely than the
    carrots
2 cups boiling water

1¾ teaspoons salt
 ½ teaspoon black pepper
  1 teaspoon powdered beef stock *or* 1 bouillon cube
  1 cup water from the vegetables

Since the meat mixture has to stand overnight, the pastry can be made the following day or it can be made and refrigerated overnight too, to be rolled out when you are ready to fill it.

In a large mixing bowl, mix the beef and onions together with the hands.

Cook the carrots and potatoes in the boiling water for about 2 minutes. Drain, and reserve 1 cup of the liquid. Add the vegetables to the meat and onion mixture.

Add the salt and pepper and dried stock to the cup of hot vegetable water and, when it has cooled a little, add it to the meat and vegetable mixture. Blend well with the hands. When the whole mixture has completely cooled, cover and refrigerate overnight.

Bang down the pastry with the rolling pin to a rectangle about 1 inch thick. Divide into four parts and refrigerate three. Roll out one section to a rectangle 4 by 16 inches. Fold up to 4 by 4 inches and roll out again. Repeat 2 to 4 times more and then roll out to 6 by 16 inches. Spread one-fourth of the meat mixture down the middle of the pastry the long way, right to the ends. Fold one side of the pastry over the meat and brush with the egg glaze. Bring the other side of the pastry over to enclose the meat, and gently press to seal. Turn the whole roll over carefully, trim the ends, and cut into four equal sections. Make two diagonal slashes on the top of each section and brush each top with egg glaze. Place about ½ inch apart on an edged cookie sheet or jelly-roll pan that has been sprinkled with flour. Roll out and fill the other sections of pastry the same way. Bake in a preheated 375° oven, 20 minutes in lower third of oven, 20 minutes in upper third, or until pastry is golden and flaky. If you have a reliable oven, another tray of pasties can be put in the lower third of the oven when the first goes to the top. Makes 16 four-inch pasties.

Pâté de Pâques
Easter Pâté in Pastry

For this pâté from the old Loire Valley province of Berry, you need a long narrow terrine or loaf pan, about 13 by 4½ by 2½ inches, holding 8 cups. This is the same amount as the regular 9-by-5-by-3-inch pan but it yields smaller, more manageable slices. Called Pâté de Pâques, Easter Pâté, it would usually be served cold in France, as a first course before an Easter dinner. Served hot, however, it would make a splendid main course for luncheon or supper, with a leafy green salad and crusty bread, and followed by fruit or sherbet. For a more substantial meal, it could be preceded by a clear soup and accompanied by a vegetable in Cream Sauce* or by Scalloped Potatoes,* and by artichokes, hot with melted butter and lemon or cold with Vinaigrette Dressing.*

Either white or red wine goes with the pâté. The white wine could be a soft Graves, a crisp Loire, or a flowery Alsatian; the red, a fresh young Beaujolais or California Pinot Noir or Gamay; a rosé would also go well with it.

Since the loaf has cheese in it, a separate cheese course is not necessary, but if you have had a red wine with the loaf, you might want to finish the wine with some more of the same cheese, Bonbel or Port Salut, along with fresh fruit.

For 8-cup loaf pan (13″ x 4½″ x 2½″)

  2 packages pie crust mix (enough for two 2-crust pies)
  ½ cup grated Bonbel or Port Salut cheese
  2 eggs, well beaten
  ¼ cup water

  1 pound lean ground pork
  1 pound lean ground veal
  ¾ pound bulk sausage meat

  2 tablespoons butter
  1 medium onion, minced
  1 clove garlic, minced

  2 eggs, well beaten
  2 teaspoons salt
  ½ teaspoon pepper
  ½ teaspoon marjoram

  6 hard-cooked eggs, halved lengthwise
  6 ounces Bonbel or Port Salut cheese, shredded

    Parsley or watercress to garnish

Mix pie crust mix with cheese. Add eggs beaten with the water. Stir until well blended and the dough cleans the bowl. Make into a ball, and, on a floured pastry cloth, knead the dough, pressing down and away from you with the heel of the hand. Reshape the ball, knead again, and repeat until the dough is smooth and elastic. Line a buttered long 8-cup pan with a piece of heavy buttered foil to cover the bottom and the two long sides, allowing 2 inches of foil to hang over the edges. This makes a kind of sling with which to remove the loaf from the pan when it is cooked. Roll out two thirds of the pastry to a rectangle 20 by 11 inches. Cut a piece of the pastry out of the center roughly the same size as the foil, to line the two long sides and the bottom, with some to hang over the edges. Cut pieces for the two small ends out of the rest of the dough, allowing for some to hang over, and enough to overlap the pastry already in the pan. Wet the overlapping edges with water and press firmly together, being careful to avoid making holes.

Mix the meats in a large bowl.

In a small heavy saucepan or skillet, melt the butter and slowly cook the onion and garlic until the onion is soft but not brown. Add to the meats.

Set aside ¼ cup of the beaten eggs for glazing the pastry. Mix the seasonings with the rest of the eggs, and beat into the meat mixture until smooth and well blended.

Spoon half of the mixture evenly into the pastry-lined pan, being careful not to make holes in the dough. Top with hard-cooked eggs, flat side down, and sprinkle cheese over them. Spread the rest of the meat mixture on top, doming it slightly down the center the long way. Turn the overhanging pastry over the meat (trim the overhang to 1 inch if necessary), and brush the pastry with beaten egg. Roll out remaining pastry and cut a rectangle 13 by 4½ inches to fit the top. Put the pastry on top of the loaf and seal the edges firmly. Make three or four 1-inch slashes in the pastry, or prick in a few places with a fork. Brush with egg, and decorate with pastry cutouts. Brush again with egg, and bake in a preheated 350° oven for 2 hours, or until pastry is richly brown. If pastry starts to brown too quickly, cover it loosely with foil for part of the time.

Once it is out of the oven, cool the loaf for 30 minutes. Check with a knife at each end to be sure the pastry is detached from the pan, and then use the overhanging foil to pull the loaf out of the pan. Slide it off the foil onto a warm platter. Surround with parsley or watercress and serve in 1-inch slices.

If loaf is to be served cold, cool to room temperature, cover, and refrigerate without removing from pan. To remove cold loaf before serving, hold pan briefly in a few inches of hot water and lift by the foil the same way as the hot loaf. Yields 10 to 12 servings.

FISH LOAVES

Saumon au Riz en Croûte
Salmon and Rice Loaf in Pastry

A pound of salmon goes a long way in this loaf, sandwiched between layers of rice, hard-cooked eggs, and a creamy sauce and wrapped in golden pastry. Accompanied by just a leafy green salad, it makes a summery luncheon or supper any time fresh salmon is available. As the main course of a more substantial meal, it could be preceded by a soup and served with a green vegetable or Celery in Egg and Lemon Sauce,* the salad then following as a separate course.

A Riesling from Alsace or the Moselle would be a marvelous white wine to have with the loaf, but a less expensive Muscadet or Sancerre from the Loire would also be good.

Baked on a cookie sheet

1 pound fresh raw salmon

1 recipe for pastry*
3 cups cooked rice, dry and cold

Salt and pepper to taste
2 cups velouté sauce
1 tablespoon chopped fresh dill *or* 1 teaspoon dried dill
1 tablespoon fresh lemon juice
3 hard-cooked eggs, finely chopped

1 egg beaten with 1 tablespoon milk for glaze

¼ pound unsalted butter, melted

Parsley (or watercress) and lemon wedges to garnish

Skin and bone the salmon, carefully removing small bones with tweezers. Cut into strips about 4 inches long and ½ inch wide.

Make velouté sauce as follows:

4 tablespoons unsalted butter
4 tablespoons flour
2 cups canned ready-to-use chicken broth
2 tablespoons dry white wine (optional)
½ cup heavy cream
Salt and pepper to taste

In a heavy saucepan, melt the butter and stir in the flour. Remove from the heat and whisk in the chicken broth. When the mixture is smooth, put it back on the heat and bring to a boil, stirring constantly. Cook over very low heat for 15 minutes, stirring almost constantly to prevent burning and to keep it smooth. Add the wine, if used, and stir in the cream. Add salt and pepper to taste. Cool, stirring occasionally, to prevent skin from forming or to incorporate it if it does. Sauce should be very thick.

Lightly butter and flour a cookie sheet. Divide the pastry in two parts. Roll out one half to ¼-inch thickness, drape over the rolling pin, and place on the cookie sheet. Trim to a rectangle 7 by 14 inches. Put a layer of rice ⅓ inch deep on the pastry, leaving a 1½-inch border all around. Sprinkle lightly with salt and pepper. Carefully spoon half the velouté sauce over the rice. Lay the salmon slices over the sauce to cover. Sprinkle with salt and pepper, dill, and lemon juice. Cover with the rest of the velouté sauce, and then the chopped eggs. Top with another ⅓-inch layer of rice, and a sprinkle of salt and pepper. Paint the border of the pastry with the egg and milk glaze.

Roll out the other half of the pastry to ¼-inch thickness. Trim to 9 by 16 inches, drape over the rolling pin, and place over the loaf. Carefully press the pastry around the loaf without stretching it. Press the edges together, and trim to about an inch around the loaf. Press the edges with the tines of a fork or make diagonal scorings with the back of a knife, being careful not to make holes in the pastry. Cut two small holes in the top of the loaf, about ½ inch in diameter, so melted butter can be poured in later. Gather scraps of pastry together and cut circles, leaf shapes, or strips for decoration. Paint entire loaf with egg and milk glaze, and stick on the decorations, then glaze the decorative pieces. Place in a preheated 400° oven and immediately turn down to 375°. Bake for 1 to 1¼ hours or until pastry is golden brown.

Remove from the oven and allow to stand for 15 minutes. Slide the loaf onto a warm platter, and pour 2 tablespoons of melted butter into each hole in the top, saving the rest to serve in a small bowl with each serving. Surround the loaf with parsley sprigs or watercress and lemon wedges. Cut into 1-inch slices. Serves 6 to 8.

This loaf can be reheated. Place uncovered in a preheated 350° oven for 20 to 30 minutes or until the crust has become tender again. The inside may not be hot, but it will have lost its chill. For a change of sauce, mix a cup of sour cream with lemon juice, dill, and salt and pepper to taste.

Ham and Clam Loaf

Ham and clams turn out to have an unexpected affinity for each other. The clams add an indefinable, light, unfishy taste to the ham, and they disappear in the attractive pink slices, which show hard-cooked egg in their centers. Seasoning is adjusted to the saltiness of the ham.

The ham can be leftovers from a baked ham or a piece bought especially for the loaf. If you get a slice from a fully cooked ham with the bone in the middle and a lot of fat around the edges, buy 1¼ pounds to allow for trimming. If it is cut from a boned, pressed piece with no fat, buy 1 pound. Packaged sliced ham will not do.

Scalloped Potatoes* and a green vegetable would be good with the loaf, and perhaps a salad of grapefruit, watercress, and avocado. The light and lovely Horseradish Sauce* is particularly right for it, and a little Dijon or Düsseldorf mustard could be around too.

Beer is always fine with ham, but, for those who prefer wine, a Sancerre from the Loire or a Chardonnay from California would be good, and a classic with ham is a Pouilly-Fuissé.

For 9"–10" baking dish

1 eight-ounce can minced clams, drained, juice reserved
1 pound lean cooked ham (about 3 cups ground)
¾ cup unsalted matzo meal
2 tablespoons finely chopped fresh parsley
¼ teaspoon freshly ground black pepper

1 egg
¾ cup milk
½ cup juice from the clams, well strained

3 hard-cooked eggs
2 tablespoons melted unsalted butter

Parsley sprigs to garnish

After draining the clams and reserving the juice, rinse the clams under cold running water, feeling them with the fingers to be sure there is no sand in them. Grind the clams with the ham and place in a large mixing bowl. Add the matzo meal, parsley, and pepper.

Lightly beat the egg and mix with the milk and clam juice. (The clam juice should be strained through a strainer lined with a dampened kitchen towel to remove any sand.) Add to the contents of the large mixing bowl and mix thoroughly. Taste and add salt if needed.

Cut a small slice off each end of each egg so they will fit together in a line. Oil a 9-to-10-inch baking dish and spread a third of the mixture on the bottom in a rectangle about 8 by 4 inches. Place the eggs in a row on the meat, and cover with the rest of the mixture, patting to make a cylindrical loaf and making sure the eggs are completely covered on the ends, sides, and top. Dribble the melted butter over the loaf, spreading it with brush or fingers to cover top and sides. Bake in a preheated 350° oven for 45 minutes, or until lightly brown on top. Serve from the baking dish or transfer carefully to a warmed platter, surrounded by parsley. Serves 4 to 6.

Fiskepudding
Norwegian Fish Pudding

Norwegians evidently love nutmeg and would not think the maximum amount in this recipe too much. For those who prefer less, half the amount is suggested. The loaf is white, with a beautiful brown coating of crumbs on the outside. The pink of shrimp in the sauce that goes with it and the feathery touch of a garnish of fresh dill make it a handsome thing indeed. Another way of serving the loaf is simply to pour melted butter over it and garnish with fresh dill or parsley. This has the advantage of enhancing the brown of the crumbs on the loaf. Boiled potatoes and spinach would go well with it, or mashed potatoes and Five-Minute Carrots.* The salad could be one of beets and endive, Sweet-Sour Cucumbers,* or cucumbers in Sour Cream and Dill Sauce.*

A white wine from Burgundy, the Rhine, or the Loire would go well with the loaf, but Norwegians are just as apt to drink beer or icy aquavit with it.

The loaf can also be served cold, on lettuce leaves, with any of the same salads and with Sour Cream and Dill Sauce.*

For 5-cup loaf pan (8½″ x 4½″ x 2½″) or 4-cup mold

    1 pound haddock or cod or any lean white fish, skinned and boned
    1 cup milk
    2 tablespoons cornstarch
    2 eggs
⅛–¼ teaspoon nutmeg
    1 teaspoon salt
      Pinch of white pepper
    1 tablespoon soft butter

    1 cup heavy cream

    1 tablespoon soft butter
    2 tablespoons fine dry bread crumbs

    Parsley sprigs and fresh dill to garnish

Cut the fish into small pieces and put into the blender. Add the milk, cornstarch, eggs, nutmeg, salt, pepper, and soft butter. Blend on high speed, stopping the machine and scraping down the sides of the jar every few seconds.

Stop the blender and pour in the cream. Blend just to incorporate the cream, stopping the machine and scraping down periodically if necessary.

Butter a loaf pan or mold, and sprinkle in the bread crumbs, shaking and turning the pan to coat with the crumbs. Discard crumbs that do not adhere. Pour in the contents of the blender and bang the pan or mold sharply on the table to get rid of any air holes. Set in a larger shallow baking dish with hot water to come halfway up the sides of the pan or mold. Place in a preheated 325° oven for 1 hour, or until a metal skewer comes out clean after being plunged into the center of the loaf.

Allow the loaf to stand for 5 minutes before unmolding. To unmold, run a knife around the loaf, place a warmed platter over the top, and invert onto the platter.

Pour Shrimp Sauce (given below) or melted butter over the loaf, surround with parsley sprigs, and top with sprigs of fresh dill. Serve extra sauce in a small bowl. Serves 4 or, with the Shrimp Sauce, 6. As a first course, the loaf will serve 8.

Shrimp Sauce

4 tablespoons butter
4 tablespoons flour
2 cups bottled clam juice
½ cup heavy cream
2 tablespoons Amontillado Sherry
¼ teaspoon white pepper
1 pound medium shrimp, cooked and chopped into ½-inch pieces
1 tablespoon finely chopped fresh dill *or* 1 teaspoon dried dill

In a 1½- to 2-quart saucepan over moderate heat, melt the butter and stir in the flour. Remove from the heat and whisk in the clam juice. Cook over low heat, stirring constantly, until the sauce is thick and smooth. Stir in the cream, Sherry, and pepper, add the shrimp, and heat just until the shrimp are heated through.

Tuna Loaf

This light and lovely loaf is adapted from *How to Eat Better for Less Money* by James A. Beard and Sam Aaron, where it is called Tuna Pudding. A perfect luncheon or supper dish, it is good hot or cold. Served hot, it is complemented by Celery in Egg and Lemon Sauce,* a leafy green salad, and crusty bread. Cold, it could be accompanied by a crisp creamy salad of cucumbers and radishes in a Sour Cream and Dill Sauce.* A white wine such as a Muscadet or a Chardonnay would be good to drink with it, or a California Grignolino or Grenache Rosé.

For 4-cup mold or 5-cup loaf pan

4–5 slices firm white home-style bread, crusts removed
  1 small can evaporated milk (¾ cup)
 ¼ cup dry white wine
  2 cups drained, flaked, water-packed white meat tuna (two 6½- or 7-ounce cans)
  1 small onion, finely chopped
 ⅓ cup finely chopped green pepper
  2 tablespoons finely chopped pimientos
    Salt and freshly ground black pepper
  3 eggs, separated

Lemon slices and chopped parsley to garnish

Make bread crumbs by tearing each slice into 4 or 5 pieces and blending a few at a time in the blender. If a blender is not available, allow the slices to dry out a bit and rub them through a sieve. Soak the bread crumbs in the milk for a few minutes, then combine with the wine, tuna, onion, green pepper, and pimientos. Mix well and add salt and pepper to taste. Beat the egg yolks and mix in. Stiffly beat the egg whites and fold in. Pour into an oiled 4-cup mold or 5-cup loaf pan, set in a larger pan of warm water, and bake in a preheated 350° oven for 50 minutes. Remove and allow to stand for 5 minutes before unmolding on a warm platter. Garnish with very thin lemon slices sprinkled with parsley. Serves 4.

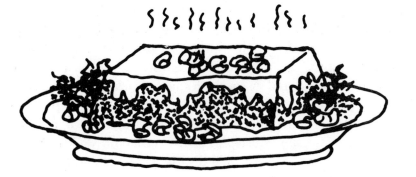

MEAT LOAVES

Pork and Sausage Loaf

This flavorful loaf, quite presentable for guests, as well as being
fine family fare, lends itself to a variety of presentations. Onions
in Cream Sauce* go particularly well with it, with some of the
sauce spooned over the slices. With this, spinach or broccoli would
be good for color and taste, and the salad could be a nice cool one
of fresh grapefruit sections with endive and watercress in a French
Dressing.* A Creamy Mustard,* Sour Cream,* or Madeira Sauce*
with sautéed mushrooms would also be good with it, along with
parsleyed potatoes and a green vegetable. Or it could have a Tomato
with Horseradish Sauce* on it and creamy macaroni to go with it,
a big green salad taking the place of a hot vegetable.

The loaf is also good cold, for buffet, picnic, or sandwiches, with a
sauce made of sour cream with some horseradish mixed in, or
mayonnaise with some Dijon mustard added.

Any dry white wine will go with the loaf, as will a light young red,
such as one from Southern Burgundy or the Rhône.

For 8-cup loaf pan (9" x 5" x 3")

- 2 pounds lean ground pork
- ¾ pound sausage
- 1 slice bacon, diced
- 1 clove garlic, minced
  Grated rind of 1 lemon
- ¼ cup finely chopped fresh parsley

- 4–5 slices firm white home-style bread, crusts removed
- ⅓ cup chicken broth

- 2 eggs
- 3 tablespoons Cognac
- 1¼ teaspoons salt
- ½ teaspoon freshly ground black pepper
  Large pinch each of sage, savory, thyme, crumbled rosemary

  Bacon strips to cover

Put the ground pork, sausage (with casings, if any, removed), diced bacon, garlic, lemon rind, and parsley into a large mixing bowl and mix lightly.

Coarsely crumble the bread, or tear it into small pieces, to make 2 cups. Moisten with the broth and add to the meats.

Lightly beat the eggs, add the Cognac and seasonings, and combine with the meats, mixing thoroughly to blend seasonings evenly through the loaf. Allow to stand for an hour.

Stir again and pack into a buttered 8-cup loaf pan, pressing into corners and patting to avoid air holes. Mound the top slightly and cover with bacon slices. Bake, uncovered, in a preheated 350° oven for 1¼ to 1½ hours, or until loaf has shrunk a little from the sides of the pan and the edges are slightly brown.

Allow loaf to stand for 5 to 10 minutes, pour off juices, and slide out, right side up, onto a warm platter.

Turkey and Ham Loaf

When everyone has had enough turkey sandwiches, one last hot meal with what is left finishes off the bird with a flourish.

The ham should be leftovers from a baked ham, or sliced from a good delicatessen boiled or baked ham, or a piece cut from a fully cooked ham steak, trimmed of fat and bone. One tightly packed cup of chopped ham is about ½ pound of ham.

The loaf can be served with leftover gravy or a cream sauce, and—for a change from cranberries—Cumberland Sauce* or chutney. Our favorite vegetable with the loaf is a mixture of mashed potatoes and yellow turnips from the original dinner, fried with onions and parsley—and a green vegetable—a brand new feast, reminiscent of but different from the original. A leafy salad or one of thinly sliced cucumbers, green onions, and parsley in French Dressing* would be good to follow, and butter pecan ice cream with honey and Sherry poured over would make a festive finish.

Beer or ale is good with this, or a Bordeaux regional red or white wine—Bordeaux Supérieur or Graves.

For 8-cup loaf pan (9" x 5" x 3")

  2 cups cooked turkey, chopped
  2 cups cooked ham, chopped

  1 tablespoon butter
½ cup finely chopped onion
  1 cup finely chopped celery
½ cup finely chopped fresh parsley

  2 cups herb-seasoned stuffing croutons *or* herb-seasoned coarse
    crumbs
½ cup chicken broth

⅛ teaspoon savory
⅛ teaspoon sage
⅛ teaspoon thyme
  2 tablespoons Amontillado Sherry
½ cup heavy cream
  3 eggs, beaten
    Salt and pepper to taste

Put the turkey and ham into a large mixing bowl.

In a heavy saucepan or skillet, melt the butter and cook the onion, celery, and parsley until the onion is limp and the celery a little transparent.

Turn off heat and stir in the crumbs, tossing to mix. Pour in the chicken broth, and add the whole mixture to the turkey and ham.

Sprinkle in the seasonings, add the wine, cream, and eggs, and mix lightly but well. Taste and add salt carefully. (The amount will depend on how salty the ham is and how much salt is in the broth and the seasoned crumbs; same with the pepper.)

Pack into a well-buttered 8-cup loaf pan, being careful to avoid air holes. Set the pan in a larger shallow pan with hot water to come halfway up the side of the loaf pan, and place in a preheated 350° oven, uncovered, for 50 to 60 minutes, or until loaf is set in the center and browning lightly around the edges and a metal skewer plunged into the middle comes out clean. Allow to stand for 5 minutes, then run a knife around the edges and invert onto a warm platter. Serves 6.

Pork and Spinach Loaf

Turned out on a platter, bottom side up, this handsome loaf hardly needs the sprinkle of parsley on top. The stripes of the bacon, and the mottle of green in the slices when it is cut, are decoration enough, except for some parsley sprigs or watercress to surround it. However, if the look of the cooked but unbrowned bacon does not appeal to you, turn the loaf right side up to show the browned bacon. Onions, Potatoes, or Celery in Cream Sauce,* with a little of the sauce served on the slices, would go well with it, and because a green vegetable is in the loaf, Five-Minute Carrots,* grilled tomatoes, or beets would make attractive second vegetables. These three vegetables also make appropriate salads for the loaf. Choose one to make that you are not serving hot: Grated Carrot Salad,* tomatoes with red onion rings, or beets with endive.

Madeira Sauce,* with or without mushrooms, would also be good with the loaf, echoing the Madeira in it. In this case, parsleyed or mashed potatoes could take the place of the vegetables in cream sauce.

A full Burgundy—a Nuits-St.-Georges or Beaune—would be splendid with the loaf but rather expensive. A less expensive choice could be California Mountain Red or a Spanish Rioja.

For 5-cup loaf pan (8½″ x 4½″ x 2½″)

1½ pounds ground pork shoulder
  2 packages frozen chopped spinach, thawed, drained, and squeezed dry

  2 tablespoons butter
  2 tablespoons flour
  ¾ cup milk

  1 egg
  2 tablespoons Madeira
1½ teaspoons salt
  ¼ teaspoon freshly ground black pepper
  ¼ teaspoon thyme
  ⅛ teaspoon mace
  ⅛ teaspoon allspice
  1 clove garlic, minced
  Grated rind of 1 lemon
  ½ cup shelled pistachio nuts, or pine nuts (optional)

  Bacon slices for top and bottom of loaf

  Parsley sprigs or watercress to garnish

Mix the pork and spinach together in a large mixing bowl.

Pork and Spinach Loaf / 167

In a small saucepan, melt the butter and stir in the flour. Remove from the heat and add the milk. Mix with a fork until smooth, and cook over low flame, stirring constantly, until it thickens. It should be very thick. Cool slightly and mix with the pork and spinach.

In a small bowl, lightly beat the egg and stir in the Madeira, seasonings, garlic, and lemon rind. Add to the pork and spinach and beat with a wooden spoon until the mixture dries a little; then mix with the hands to be sure ingredients are well blended. Stir in the nuts, if used.

Line the bottom of a 5-cup loaf pan with slices of bacon and put in the meat mixture, pressing into corners and patting to avoid air holes. Cover the loaf completely with bacon slices and bake, uncovered, in a 350° oven for 1¼ hours, or until the loaf has shrunk from the sides of the pan a bit and a metal skewer pushed into the center comes out clean.

Allow the loaf to stand for about 10 minutes. With a spatula, gently move it from side to side and end to end of the pan to be sure it is free from the bottom. Holding the loaf with the spatula, tip the pan to pour off juices, then turn out onto a warm platter. Wipe the edges of the platter clean, and surround with parsley or watercress. Serves 4 to 6.

Pork and Apple Loaf

Moist and interestingly flavored, this loaf is light enough for a luncheon, accompanied just by a salad, and substantial enough for dinner with perhaps parsleyed potatoes and broccoli. Apples con-

tribute to the moistness, and sweet Vermouth is an unusual accent. Onions in Cream Sauce* are suggested to provide both a sauce for the loaf and an extra vegetable.

We like this loaf in our house and have a lot of suggestions for drinkables to go with it. Cider, hard or sweet, is good, because of the apples in the loaf, and so is beer, or chilled Fino or Manzanilla Sherry. Any of the inexpensive red or white wines suggested throughout the book would be fine, but, for the adventurous, some wines with special tastes might be explored: Delaware or Lake Country White from New York State, the straw wines of the Savoie (ask for them as such in specialty wine shops), or Hungarian reds or whites.

For 8"–10" oval or rectangular nonmetallic baking dish

1½ pounds ground pork shoulder
 1 medium onion, finely chopped
 1 clove garlic, smashed and minced
 ⅓ cup coarsely chopped walnuts (¼-inch pieces)
 1 teaspoon grated lemon rind
 2 medium apples, peeled, cored, and finely chopped (2 cups)
 2 tablespoons lemon juice

3–4 slices firm white home-style bread, crusts removed
 ¼ cup sweet Vermouth

 2 eggs
1½ teaspoons salt
 ¼ teaspoon freshly ground black pepper
 ¼ teaspoon rosemary, crumbled
 ⅛ teaspoon thyme
 ⅛ teaspoon sage, crumbled
 ⅛ teaspoon nutmeg

   Chopped parsley to garnish

Put the pork, onion, garlic, walnuts, lemon rind, and apples in a large mixing bowl, with the apples on top. Sprinkle lemon juice over all and mix lightly.

Coarsely crumble the bread, or tear it into small pieces, to make 1½ cups. Soak it in the Vermouth for a few minutes and add to the meat mixture.

Lightly beat the eggs and add the seasonings. Mix thoroughly with the rest of the ingredients.

Mold the mixture into a loaf about 8 inches long and 4 inches wide. Place in an oiled nonmetallic baking dish and set in a preheated 350° oven. Cook, uncovered, for 1 to 1¼ hours, or until juices run clear when loaf is pricked and pressed and the top is brown.

Remove from the oven and allow to stand for 10 minutes. Pour off fat. Serve in baking dish, or slide out onto a hot platter. If served with Onions in Cream Sauce,* the sauce can be poured over the loaf and the onions placed around it, with a sprinkling of parsley over all. Serves 4 to 5.

Middle Eastern Lamb Loaf

Well-spiced and shaped like a giant hamburger, this loaf is cooked under the broiler for only 15 to 20 minutes, so have the accompanying vegetables almost ready when the loaf is put in to cook. Lemon Rice,* with or without raisins, is very good to serve with it, along with fried zucchini or eggplant and a green salad or sliced tomatoes. Or the zucchini could be used in salad instead of cooked—sliced thinly with tomatoes and Vinaigrette Dressing.* Beer goes well with all this, or a hearty inexpensive red wine, like a Spanish Rioja or an American jug wine.

For 9″ pie plate, or on foil, to go under the broiler

1½ pounds ground lean lamb
½ pound ground beef chuck
2–3 slices firm white home-style bread, crusts removed
2 tablespoons finely chopped fresh parsley
1 large clove garlic, minced

1 egg
2 tablespoons tomato paste mixed with 2 tablespoons water
1 teaspoon ground cumin
1½ teaspoons salt
⅛ teaspoon cayenne pepper, or to taste
1 teaspoon dried mint, crumbled
½ teaspoon ground coriander
½ teaspoon oregano

Parsley sprigs or watercress to garnish

Put the meats in a large mixing bowl. Coarsely crumble the bread, or tear it into small pieces to make 1 cup. Add to the meat. Add the parsley and garlic and mix lightly.

In a small bowl, lightly beat the egg and add the tomato paste and water. Stir in the seasonings and add to the meat mixture. Mix well with the hands and form into a flat round loaf, about 8 inches in diameter and about 1½ inches deep. Place in an oiled 9-inch pie plate, or on a piece of heavy foil with the edges turned up to catch any fat. Preheat the broiler and place the loaf about 3 inches under the flame. Cook for 7 to 10 minutes, until the top is well browned. Turn over carefully with two spatulas and cook until that side is brown. Loaf should be slightly pink in the center.

Slide onto a hot platter and surround with parsley sprigs or watercress. Serve in wedges, like a pie. Serves 4.

A Restricted Veal Loaf

This strangely named loaf caught my eye when I was going through one of my favorite "reading" cookbooks, *The Alice B. Toklas Cook Book.* This recipe comes from the section of the book where Miss Toklas describes the way she and Gertrude Stein lived in the French countryside during the German occupation of World War II. Meat was very scarce, eggs were rare, but wine and herbs were plentiful since they were lucky enough to have a wine cellar and an herb garden. So the loaf is "restricted" in the use of meat, with only ½ pound to 3 cups of bread crumbs, and only one precious egg, but plenty of flavor is supplied by dry white wine and an unusual group of herbs. Since we are more likely to be short of wine, and to make it even easier to cook, we have added strips of bacon on the top to obviate the need for basting with wine. We have also added some salt, which is not mentioned in the recipe.

A tiny loaf, it is enough for two people, served with a green vegetable and a salad, but it might be stretched for three if it were preceded by a first course, and accompanied by parsleyed or Scalloped Potatoes* as well as the green vegetable. The dry white wine used in the cooking would be a good one to have with the loaf— a Muscadet or Chardonnay.

For 8″–9″ nonmetallic baking dish

½ pound ground veal
2 small onions, finely chopped (about 1 cup)
2 tablespoons shallots, minced, *or* 1 small clove garlic, minced
1 tablespoon finely chopped fresh parsley

6–7 slices firm white home-style bread, crusts removed
½ cup dry white wine

1 egg
½ teaspoon salt
¼ teaspoon freshly ground black pepper
½ teaspoon basil
½ teaspoon tarragon
½ teaspoon chervil
1 medium bay leaf, finely crumbled

2 slices bacon, to top loaf

Parsley sprigs or watercress to garnish

In a large mixing bowl, combine the veal, onions, shallots, and parsley.

Coarsely crumble the bread, or tear it into small pieces, to make 3 cups. Soak the bread in the wine for a few minutes and add to the mixing bowl.

In a small bowl, beat the egg and add the seasonings. Add to the other ingredients and mix thoroughly. Form into a loaf about 7 inches long and 3 inches wide and place in a buttered nonmetallic baking dish. Cover with bacon and place in a preheated 375° oven for 1 hour.

Cool for 15 minutes and serve from the baking dish, or remove to a warm platter. Surround with parsley or watercress. Serves 2 to 3.

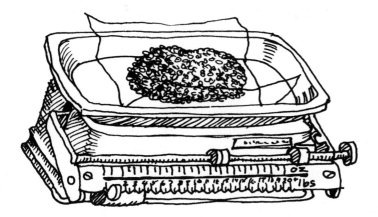

STUFFED MEATS

Matambre
Stuffed Rolled Beef Loaf

A sort of *ballottine* in France, or *braciola* in Italy, this version of beef, spread with goodies and rolled jelly-roll fashion, is Argentinian. The name Matambre, from *mata hambre*, means it kills hunger, and this good beef roll, they say, was carried across the pampas by stagecoach travelers to see them through the journey. This means that it can be eaten cold, and perhaps usually was, but it makes a wonderful hot dish, with rice or beans and its own fine hot chili sauce.

Beer goes well with this, or any dry red wine, particularly one from the Rioja in Spain or those of Chile or the Argentine.

For large, lidded casserole or roasting pan

2 flank steaks, about 2 pounds each, butterflied
1 cup dry red wine
1 clove garlic, minced

1 teaspoon thyme
½ teaspoon salt

½ pound fresh spinach
 2 medium carrots, cut in 6 lengthwise strips
 1 green pepper, in ¼-inch lengthwise strips
 3 hard-cooked eggs, in lengthwise quarters
¼ cup pimientos, in strips
 1 medium onion, thinly sliced in rings
 2 tablespoons chopped fresh parsley
½ teaspoon red pepper flakes or more, to taste
 2 teaspoons salt
½ teaspoon freshly ground black pepper

   Marinade liquid
 3 cans ready-to-use beef broth (13¾-ounce size)
 1 medium onion, quartered
 1 celery stalk, cut in 2 pieces
 1 medium carrot, sliced
   Water to barely cover
   Salt and pepper to taste

Most butchers will butterfly the steaks for you. If not, it is done by slicing the steaks horizontally from one long side to within half an inch of the opposite side, then opening them out like a butterfly. They are now twice as large and half as thick. Pound them between sheets of waxed paper to make them uniformly thin. Trim off gristle and fat.

Spread out one steak, cut side up, in a nonmetallic baking dish or shallow serving dish. Sprinkle it with half each of the wine, the garlic, the thyme and the salt. Lay the other steak on top and sprinkle it with the rest of the wine, garlic, thyme, and salt. Cover and allow to stand (marinate) for several hours, or overnight in the refrigerator.

Remove the steaks, reserving the marinade, and spread them out, with a short side of one overlapping a short side of the other by about 2 inches. Pound the overlap to seal and make it thinner.

Wash, drain, and trim the stems from the spinach. Spread it evenly over the meat. Lay the carrot strips across in parallel rows about 3 inches apart. Spread the green pepper strips between the rows and place the egg sections on them. Scatter the pimientos and onion rings over them, and spread parsley, red pepper flakes, salt, and pepper evenly over all.

The trick now is to roll up the meat, jelly-roll fashion, with all its filling. Make the first turn quite firm, and continue rolling as firmly as possible, tucking in bits that fall out of the ends, until you are approaching the overlap of the two steaks. When the overlap is visible on the bottom of the roll, you may want to stick a few toothpicks straight in, about halfway, to hold the meat together until the seam is on the top of the roll. Remove the toothpicks and continue rolling, holding the seam together until you have rolled past it. Roll to the end, tuck in scraggly bits at the sides, and tie with string at 2-inch intervals and, if necessary, once the long way too.

Place the roll in a large, lidded casserole or roasting pan, preferably oval. Add the marinade juices and the rest of the poaching stock ingredients—beef broth, onion, celery, carrot, and water—with salt and pepper to taste. Bring to a boil, reduce the heat, and simmer, partially covered, for 1½ hours, or until tender. Turn the roll carefully at least once during cooking.

Remove the roll to a hot platter and keep warm while you make the chili sauce. Save the stock; you will need 1 cup for this sauce, and leftover stock can be frozen for other uses.

2 tablespoons butter
1 small onion, finely chopped
1 clove garlic, minced
1 tablespoon flour
1 tablespoon chili powder
1 teaspoon salt
¼ teaspoon freshly ground black pepper
1 cup tomato juice
1 cup stock from the poaching of the Matambre

To make chili sauce, melt the butter in a heavy saucepan and slowly cook the onion and garlic until the onion is limp but not brown. Stir in the flour, chili powder, salt, and pepper. Add the tomato juice and stock, and cook, stirring, until sauce is smooth and slightly thickened.

To serve the Matambre hot, stick toothpicks into the roll at half-inch intervals before removing the string, to keep the slices from coming apart. Remove the string and slice the roll between the toothpicks, arranging the slices with a cake knife or spatula so they overlap slightly. Remove toothpicks and moisten slices with some of the stock. Serve the hot chili sauce in a bowl, to be used on individual servings. Serves 8.

If the Matambre is to be served cold, allow it to come to room temperature with the strings still on, wrap in foil, and refrigerate. When it is cold, remove strings and slice in quarter-inch slices.

Morcon
Philippine Rolled Stuffed Beef

Another version of the stuffed roll of beef is this one from the Philippines. We are not prepared to swear to its authenticity, only to its good taste, as worked out from available clues. The Philippine cuisine is a combination of Chinese and Spanish influences. The Chinese is understandable, but the Spanish is a surprise unless you remember that there were four centuries of Spanish colonial rule before the American period. This rolled beef reflects the Chinese aspect in the use of soy sauce, garlic, and scallions; it is Spanish in its chorizo (Spanish sausage) and the piquant tomato sauce it is cooked in. Chorizo is available in Spanish and Mexican markets, where they exist; if it is not to be found, some other highly seasoned garlic sausage can be substituted.

In the Philippines, the morcon might be one of several main-course dishes, in the Chinese fashion. To make it the center of a more

European meal, it could be preceded by an antipasto, accompanied by spinach and plain rice, Risotto,* or noodles, and followed by a goat cheese and stewed apricots or fresh pineapple.

Because of the vinegar in the sauce, the morcon needs a hearty wine, a Spanish red like Rioja or a Bordeaux regional—Haut-Médoc, . Margaux, St. Julien, or St. Estèphe.

For heavy covered casserole

  1 flank steak, 2½–3 pounds, butterflied
  3 tablespoons lemon juice
  3 tablespoons soy sauce

  2 cloves garlic, minced
  2 medium carrots, each in 6 lengthwise strips
 ½ pound chorizo (Spanish sausage) *or* other highly seasoned
    garlic sausage, in strips
4–6 scallions, in lengthwise strips
  3 hard-cooked eggs, in lengthwise quarters

  2 tablespoons olive oil
  1 medium onion, minced
  2 cups water
  1 one-pound can tomatoes, sieved
 ¼ cup vinegar
  1 bay leaf
    Salt and pepper to taste

If the butcher won't butterfly the steak, you can do it yourself. Slice the steak horizontally from one long side to within ½ inch of the other side. Spread the steak open like a butterfly, and pound it between two pieces of waxed paper, with a rolling pin or the edge of a bread board, until it is as thin and even as possible.

Lay the steak, cut side up, in a shallow roasting pan or edged cookie sheet. Rub in a tablespoon each of lemon juice and soy sauce, and pour the rest over the steak. Allow to stand for about an hour.

Pour off and reserve any juices from the steak, and scatter the garlic evenly over it. Lay the carrot strips in parallel rows across the grain. Between the rows, place the sausage strips, scallions, and eggs. Roll up the steak and its filling like a jelly roll, gently but firmly. Stick a few toothpicks in the roll to hold it together while you tie it at 2-inch intervals with string.

Heat the oil in a heavy, lidded casserole, preferably oval, that will just take the roll. Pat the roll dry, remove the toothpicks, and brown it lightly on all sides. Put in the onion and allow to cook for a moment or two, but not long enough to brown. Add the water, tomatoes, vinegar, and reserved juices from the marinating. Add the bay leaf, salt and pepper to taste, and bring to a boil. Turn down to a simmer, cover, and cook for 1½ hours or until tender. Turn the roll about three times during cooking.

To serve, remove the roll from the pan to a cutting board. Stick a few toothpicks in at intervals to hold it together, and remove string. Slice in ¾-inch slices, and arrange them, overlapping slightly, on a heated platter, using a cake knife or wide spatula. Remove toothpicks. Skim fat from the sauce the roll was cooked in and discard. Check seasoning of the sauce and serve separately in a bowl. Serves 6 to 8.

Boned and prepared for stuffing like a galantine (page 105), this chicken is roasted, rather than poached, and served hot. The stuffing is a well-seasoned bread one and will please those who feel there is never enough in a small chicken, but the thing that distinguishes the dish is that the chicken meat and skin are marinated in Cognac and Madeira for several hours. A carver's delight, with no carcass bones, it can have two or three slices cut from the middle, and the rest cut to make two portions with wings and two with drumsticks. For those partial to breast meat, the breast of another chicken can be skinned, boned, and added to the original.

The recipe includes a stock made from the bones and giblets of the chicken, with which a gravy can be made. The gravy is nice to have if the bird is to be served with mashed potatoes, rice, or noodles. Cumberland Sauce* or chutney would go well, too. Braised endive or celery would make a good second vegetable, with cold artichokes and French* or Vinaigrette Dressing* for salad. Roquefort cheese and apples, or Boursault with good ripe pears, would make an easy and excellent dessert.

This is a loaf that my husband particularly likes, and, although a fine Chardonnay from California is very good with it, he gets excited about the possibilities of more expensive wines. For whites, he suggests a Corton Charlemagne or Chassagne-Montrachet from Burgundy; for reds, a château-bottled St. Émilion or Pomerol or an estate-bottled Volnay or Beaune. Since chickens are relatively inexpensive, and this version is so glamorous, you might want to make it very special by serving a wonderful wine.

For shallow open roasting pan with rack

- 1 roasting chicken, 3½ pounds
- 2 tablespoons Cognac
- ¼ teaspoon thyme
- ⅛ teaspoon allspice
- ¼ teaspoon salt
- ¼ teaspoon freshly ground black pepper
- 1 tablespoon Madeira

Bone the chicken as described in the directions for Galantines, reserving the bones and giblets for stock.

Spread out the chicken skin, flesh side up, on a small deep platter, nonmetallic baking dish, or bowl, with the legs and wings hanging over the edge. Place the slices of breast and all white meat (about 1 cup) in the middle of the skin. Sprinkle with half each of the Cognac, thyme, allspice, salt, and pepper. Fold the drumsticks, wings, and skin over to cover. Put the rest of the meat of the chicken (about 1 cup) on top and sprinkle with the other half of the Cognac and seasonings. Sprinkle the Madeira over all. Cover and allow to stand, at room temperature, for 6 hours, or refrigerate overnight.

The stock can be prepared while the chicken is marinating, or the bones and giblets can be refrigerated for cooking later. Allow a good 2 hours for the stock to simmer before it is needed for the gravy.

Wing tips, wing and thigh bones, carcass bones (broken up), neck, liver, heart, and gizzard from the boned chicken
2 quarts water
1 small onion, halved
1 teaspoon salt
8–10 whole black peppercorns
1 bay leaf

To make stock, put bones, giblets, water, onion, salt, peppercorns, and bay leaf in a deep saucepan. Bring to a boil and boil gently for 15 to 20 minutes, removing scum as it forms. When scum has stopped forming, turn heat down to maintain a simmer. Fish out the liver and test it; it should be tender but no longer pink inside. If it needs more cooking, put it back for another 10 minutes. Then mash it with a fork, discarding gristly bits. Set the mashed liver aside, with enough stock on it to keep it moist, until it is time to make the gravy.

Simmer the stock, partially covered, for 1½ hours, or until gizzard and heart are tender. Remove gizzard and heart. Cut away gristle from gizzard and chop finely. Finely chop heart and add both to the mashed liver, with more stock to keep moist. Strain stock into another saucepan, discarding all remaining solids. Measure the stock; if it is more than 2 cups, boil down to 2 cups. Set aside until it is time to make the gravy.

When you are ready to cook the chicken, make the bread stuffing.

    2   tablespoons butter
    1   medium onion, finely chopped
    1   cup finely chopped celery
    ¼   cup finely chopped parsley
        Salt and freshly ground pepper, to taste
    ¼   teaspoon marjoram
    ¼   teaspoon thyme
        Pinch of sage
    2   cups herb-seasoned coarse stuffing crumbs
    1   teaspoon Bell's poultry seasoning
    1   egg, lightly beaten

    2   tablespoons soft butter, to coat the chicken

    2   tablespoons flour, for gravy

        Parsley or watercress to garnish

In a heavy saucepan, melt the butter and add the onion, celery, and parsley. Sprinkle with salt, pepper, marjoram, thyme, and sage. Cook slowly until onion and celery are a little soft. Remove from the heat and toss with the stuffing crumbs and poultry seasoning, to mix well. Add the egg and toss again. Taste and adjust seasoning. Stuffing needs plenty of salt and pepper, and you may want more of the other seasonings, depending on the amount of seasoning in the crumbs.

Remove the cover from the marinated chicken, pour the juices into the bread stuffing, and mix well. Set aside the dark meat from the top of the chicken and open up the skin. Pile the stuffing on the breast meat and other white meat. If you have extra breast meat, press it along the sides of the stuffing. Cover with the dark meat.

Bring the skin up around the mound of meat and stuffing, and sew it all together with a needle and coarse white thread, patting and pushing into a semblance of the original shape, with the drumsticks and wings in place. Sew in large stitches, without knots, for easy removal. The chicken should not be too tightly packed, since the crumbs will expand, so it will seem a little flat, looking more like a duck than a chicken. With a brush or the fingers, spread half the soft butter over the skin, covering every reachable spot.

Carefully place the chicken, buttered side (sewn side) down, on a rack set in a shallow roasting pan. Cross the legs and tie to the tail with string. Skewer the wings to the body if necessary. Spread with the rest of the butter, covering every remaining spot.

Roast the chicken in a preheated 450° oven for 15 minutes. Turn oven down to 350° and roast for 45 to 60 minutes, or until the leg, when pricked, does not ooze pink juices, and the chicken is beautifully brown.

Transfer the chicken to a hot platter and keep it warm while the gravy is made, removing threads, trussing string, and skewer.

To make gravy, pour off all but 2 tablespoons of fat from the pan. (If there isn't enough to make 2 tablespoons, add butter.) Stir 2 tablespoons of flour into the fat in the roasting pan. Add the mashed liver and the chopped heart and gizzard. Turn heat on low under the pan and add stock gradually, stirring constantly, until you have incorporated all bits on the bottom of the pan and the gravy has thickened. Start with 1½ cups of stock and add more if a thinner gravy is desired. Serve in gravy boat or bowl.

Serve the chicken surrounded by parsley or watercress. Serves 4.

STUFFED VEGETABLES

Since this book deals with ground meat, it seems appropriate that it should include some ways of using ground meat for stuffing vegetables. Always a favorite for family meals, stuffed vegetables make a fine buffet dish too, handsome to see, when cooked in an oven-to-table baking dish, and easy to eat with a fork alone. They can serve as a main course after a pâté or be the one hot dish in an otherwise cold buffet (which could include a pâté).

Mexican Cabbage Rolls

Although these rolls have rice in them, Risotto* or plain rice is good with them, partly as a vehicle for the sauce. A thinly sliced Orange and Cucumber Salad* with chopped green onions and Boston lettuce is a marvelously fresh salad to follow.

For a buffet, the cabbage rolls can be made half as large, yielding 20 to 24. Mixing national origins to make an unusual buffet, you might serve cold Matambre (page 176) or Morcon (page 180), and the Risotto,* or a bean casserole of some kind. A big green salad, plenty of crusty bread, and a large platter of wedges of assorted kinds of melon could round out the feast. A hearty red wine from Spain, South America, or Italy, or an American jug wine, would be good to drink with the rolls, however they are used, and so would beer.

For shallow covered nonmetallic baking dish

  1 medium cabbage

½ pound ground pork
½ pound ground beef
½ cup uncooked rice
  1 small onion, chopped

  1 egg, lightly beaten
¼ cup water
½ teaspoon red pepper flakes, or to taste
½ cup grated sharp Cheddar cheese
  1 tablespoon salt
  1 clove garlic, minced

  1 large (2-pound-3-ounce) can Italian tomatoes

Trim off any bad outside leaves from the cabbage and cut out about 2 inches of the core. Immerse the head in boiling water; as soon as the outside leaves are slightly limp and can be removed, take them off with tongs and set them to drain. Remove the next leaves when they are ready, and continue until you have enough—about twelve. When the leaves get small, you may need two to equal one of the large ones. This process takes 5 to 10 minutes.

Lightly mix the meat, rice, and onion in a large mixing bowl.

In a smaller bowl, mix the egg with the water and combine with the pepper flakes, cheese, salt, and garlic. Add to the meat mixture and mix thoroughly.

Place a mound of filling on each cabbage leaf, fold the sides of the leaf over the meat, and roll up, from the base to the tip, not too tightly, to allow for the rice to expand. Secure the rolls with toothpicks. Set the rolls in one layer in a shallow nonmetallic baking dish, and pour the tomatoes over all. Cook, covered, in a preheated 325° oven for 1 hour. Serves 4 to 6.

Balkan Stuffed Eggplant

These steaming ovals of eggplant, mounded high with redolent stuffing, are practically a meal in themselves, although very small eggplants could be used, and the dish served hot or cold as a buffet item. Two versions follow, and a leafy green salad would go with either of them, but the first one, with its touch of lemon, would be enhanced by a salad of cucumbers in Sour Cream and Dill Sauce.* Crusty French or Italian bread is essential, unless you can find those round flat loaves of Syrian bread to serve hot and buttered.

For hearty appetites, here are some suggestions for starchy accompaniments: Lemon Rice,* Rice Pilaf with Almonds* with added raisins, or spaghetti sprinkled with grated Parmesan cheese, browned butter poured over.

The wine should be an inexpensive red, such as Beaujolais, Côtes du Rhône or Valpolicella, or an American jug wine, Zinfandel or Mountain Red. Fresh or stewed fruit would make a typical and appropriate dessert.

For casserole or baking dish

  2 medium eggplants (about 1 pound each)
  2 tablespoons olive oil
     Sprinkle of salt and pepper for pulp

  2 tablespoons olive oil
  1 small onion, finely chopped (about ½ cup)
  2 cloves garlic, minced
  1 pound ground lamb

  1 one-pound can Italian tomatoes
1½ teaspoons salt, or to taste
  ½ teaspoon freshly ground black pepper
  1 teaspoon oregano
  ½ teaspoon thyme
  2 tablespoons finely chopped fresh parsley
  ¼ cup uncooked rice

  2 tablespoons lemon juice
     Sprinkle of salt and pepper for shells
     Olive oil for bottom of baking dish

     Chopped parsley to garnish

Wash the eggplants and slice in half lengthwise. With a spoon, scoop out pulp, leaving a shell about ½ inch thick. Set aside the shells and coarsely chop the pulp, seeds and all. In a large, lidded skillet, preferably enameled ironware, heat the oil and quickly sauté the pulp, tossing and adding more oil if necessary. Sprinkle lightly with salt and pepper and set aside.

Wipe the skillet to remove bits of eggplant, and heat the olive oil. Slowly cook the onion and garlic until onion is soft but not brown. Crumble in the lamb and cook, stirring and breaking up the lumps, until the meat has lost its pink color and has dried a bit but is not quite brown. Turn off heat, tip the pan slightly, push the meat back from the edge, and spoon out and discard any fat that has gathered.

Put the tomatoes into a bowl and break them up with the fingers. Mix in the seasonings and the rice. Add to the meat in the skillet. Bring to a simmer, cover, and cook on a very low flame for 20 minutes.

Remove from the heat and stir in the lemon juice and the eggplant pulp. Salt and pepper the shells and fill them with stuffing. Film the bottom of a casserole or baking dish with olive oil, place the filled shells in, side by side, cover with lid or foil, and bake in a pre-heated 325° oven for 50 minutes, or until shells are tender. If the filling looks packed down after cooking, fluff gently with a fork on the tops before sprinkling with chopped parsley. Serves 4.

Italian Stuffed Eggplant

This version, served as a main course, needs only a leafy salad and crusty bread, but for hearty appetites it could be accompanied by Risotto* or Spaghetti with Garlic Sauce.* As with the Balkan version, small eggplants can be used, and served hot or cold for a buffet item, and the same wines go with it.

2 medium eggplants (about 1 pound each)
2 tablespoons olive oil
  Sprinkle of salt and pepper for pulp

2 tablespoons olive oil
1 small onion, finely chopped (about ½ cup)
2 cloves garlic, minced
1 pound lean ground beef

1 one-pound can Italian tomatoes
1 cup herb-seasoned stuffing croutons *or*
  herb-seasoned coarse crumbs
1 teaspoon salt, or to taste
½ teaspoon freshly ground black pepper
½ teaspoon oregano
½ teaspoon thyme
¼ teaspoon rosemary, crumbled
¼ cup grated Parmesan cheese

  Sprinkle of salt and pepper for shells
8 ounces sliced Mozzarella cheese (optional)
  Olive oil for bottom of baking dish

  Chopped parsley to garnish

Wash the eggplants and slice in half lengthwise. With a spoon, scoop out pulp, leaving a shell about ½ inch thick. Set aside the shells and coarsely chop the pulp, seeds and all. In a large, lidded skillet, preferably enameled ironware, heat the oil and quickly sauté the pulp, tossing and adding more oil if necessary. Sprinkle lightly with salt and pepper, and set aside.

Italian Stuffed Eggplant / 193

Wipe the skillet to remove bits of eggplant, and heat the olive oil. Slowly cook the onion and garlic until onion is soft but not brown. Crumble in the beef and cook, stirring and breaking up the lumps, until the meat has lost its pink color and has dried a bit but is not quite brown. Turn off heat, tip the pan slightly, push the meat back from the edge, and spoon out and discard any fat that has gathered.

In a large bowl, break up the tomatoes with the fingers. Add the croutons or crumbs, seasonings, reserved pulp, Parmesan cheese, and the meat mixture, and toss to mix well.

Lightly salt and pepper the shells and mound the mixture in them. Cover stuffing with Mozzarella, if used, and place the filled shells in a baking dish or casserole that has been filmed with olive oil. Cover the dish with lid or foil and bake in a preheated 325° oven for 50 minutes, or until shells are tender. Remove lid or covering foil after 30 minutes of cooking if Mozzarella is used. Sprinkle with chopped parsley. Serves 4.

Tomates Farcies
Stuffed Tomatoes

The memory of Tomates Farcies, the cheapest thing on the menu in a student restaurant in Paris years ago, prompted experiments resulting in the recipe that follows. Research revealed that those fondly remembered stuffings were made mostly of highly seasoned bread crumbs, lots of garlic, and olive oil. Since only an impecunious art student, sentimental about Paris, could find this an adequate main course, I have added some meat and a sprinkle of cheese but tried to keep the satisfying seasoning. In that French restaurant, the stuffed tomatoes were served with just a green salad and plenty of French bread, preceded by an inexpensive first course of Oeufs Durs Mayonnaise, hard-cooked eggs with mayonnaise. This combination still makes a fine luncheon or supper, with an American jug wine, Mountain White or Mountain Red, taking the place of the French carafe wine. However, for a more substantial meal, the tomatoes can be accompanied by macaroni and cheese, or a simple Spaghetti with Garlic Sauce,* and a salad of cooked green beans in French Dressing.* Also, made in the smaller size, they make a good hot buffet item. They can be prepared ahead and popped into the oven 20 to 30 minutes before serving.

For baking dish or casserole

4 large fresh tomatoes *or* 8 small ones (about 2 inches in diameter)
Sprinkle of olive oil for each shell
4 leaves fresh basil, chopped, *or* good pinch of dried basil
Salt and pepper to taste

1 tablespoon olive oil
1 small onion, finely chopped
1 large clove garlic, minced
½ pound ground beef

½ teaspoon salt
¼ teaspoon freshly ground black pepper
2 tablespoons finely chopped fresh parsley
¼ teaspoon thyme
¼ teaspoon marjoram
Pinch of rosemary, crumbled
¾ cup herb-seasoned stuffing croutons *or* large herb-seasoned bread crumbs

4 teaspoons grated Parmesan cheese
Olive oil for the bottom of the baking dish

Parsley sprigs to garnish

Cut a generous top off each tomato and reserve edible portion. Scoop out the pulp, chop with the trimmed tops, and put aside in a small bowl. Drain the shells by inverting on paper towels for a few minutes and then sprinkle the insides with olive oil, basil, and plenty of salt and pepper.

In a large skillet, preferably enameled ironware, heat the oil, and cook the onion and garlic slowly, on low heat, until the onion is soft but not brown. Add the ground beef and cook, stirring and breaking up the lumps, until the beef has just begun to brown. Remove from the heat, tip the pan slightly, push the meat away from the lower edge, and spoon out and discard the fat that gathers.

Mix remaining seasonings with the chopped tomato pulp, and stir into the beef mixture. Cook over low heat for 10 to 15 minutes, until mixture begins to dry. Stir in the bread crumbs and allow to cool slightly.

Heap the filling into the shells and sprinkle with Parmesan cheese. Pour a light film of oil onto the bottom of the baking dish or casserole, and place the stuffed tomatoes in it. Bake, uncovered, in preheated 350° oven for 20 to 30 minutes, or until the tomatoes are cooked but not collapsing. Serve hot with a sprig of parsley tucked into each. Serves 4. The small size serves 6 to 8 for a first course or buffet item.

Back of the Book
Recipes

A pastry recipe, a spice mixture, a few vegetables, salads, dressings, and sauces, and two wine punches that go particularly well with pâtés and meat loaves and the buffets built around them. They are suggested throughout the book, marked with an asterisk(*).

Pastry

½ pound butter
½ pound lard
4 cups sifted all-purpose flour
1 teaspoon salt
½ cup ice water

First, equip yourself with a pastry cloth and rolling-pin sleeve. They make the job much easier and, kept in a plastic bag, will always be ready for use.

Cut up the butter and lard into small pieces, ¼ to ½ inch, and refrigerate before beginning. This will cut down the time needed to mix the fats with the flour, and a certain amount of speed is required to do the job before the fats become oily.

Sift the flour and salt together into a wide deep bowl. Add half the butter and lard, leaving the rest in the refrigerator until needed.

Plunge the hands into the bowl and lift up some flour and fat and rub between thumbs and fingers, *away* from you, just once. Don't worry any one piece; let it go until another time around. Keep doing this, not lingering over any lumps, lifting and rubbing, until the texture is like coarse flakes. Add the rest of the butter and lard and continue, trying to incorporate all the flour and breaking up the butter and lard into smaller and smaller pieces. Do this as quickly as you can, and consider it done when there is practically no plain, powdery flour left and there are no huge chunks of butter or lard, although there may be some variety in the size of the pieces. Remove material stuck to the hands by rubbing with a little fresh flour, letting what comes off fall into the bowl.

Add the water all at once, toss with a fork, and then gather up into a ball. If it crumbles, add more water, 1 teaspoon at a time, until particles adhere. Don't add more water than absolutely necessary. Dust with flour and pat into a rectangle, smoothing any cracks, and wrap in waxed paper. Refrigerate for about ½ hour, just long enough to firm it up a little but not so much that it won't give to a gentle poke with a finger. The length of time needed to firm the pastry will depend on how soft the butter and lard have become during the blending. It can be refrigerated, well wrapped, for as long as several days before rolling out, but will then have to be left out to soften a bit before being used. If it crumbles and breaks, let it warm up a little longer. For longer storage, pastry can be frozen.

When you are ready to use the pastry, rub flour into the pastry cloth and rolling-pin sleeve. Lightly flour the pastry and bang it down with the pin to a 1-inch-thick rectangle. Roll out on the pastry cloth with short rolls, from the center to the top or bottom, and from the center to each side, pressing lightly and shaping as you go, as directed in the recipe for the loaf you are making. If holes or splits occur, patch with a scrap of pastry and roll over it.

For a flakier pastry, roll it out a little smaller or thinner than called for, fold it over on itself to make 3 or 4 layers and roll out again. Repeat this process two to four times and then roll out to required size or thickness.

Quatre-Épices (Four Spices)

7 tablespoons whole white peppercorns
1 tablespoon whole cloves
1 tablespoon ground dried ginger
1 tablespoon ground nutmeg

Combine ingredients in a blender and blend until smooth. This makes about ¾ cup. Keep in a sealed jar.

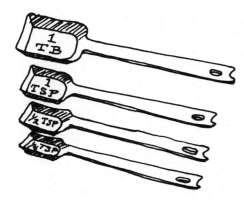

VEGETABLES AND
STARCHY ACCOMPANIMENTS

Potatoes, Onions, or Celery in Cream Sauce

This recipe makes ample sauce, of the right texture, to pour over a hot meat loaf and use for vegetables for 4 to 6. When sauce is not to be put on the loaf, it is enough for vegetables for 8. The vegetables are cooked separately and added to the sauce. Both sauce and vegetables can be done ahead and warmed up in a chafing dish at the table; some of the sauce can be spooned over the whole loaf, or served on individual slices.

3 tablespoons butter
3 tablespoons flour
3 cups milk
    Salt, pepper, and nutmeg to taste
3 tablespoons finely chopped fresh parsley

Melt the butter, stir in the flour, remove from the heat, and stir in the milk. When the sauce is smooth, put back on the heat and cook, stirring, until it comes to a boil and thickens. Add salt, pepper, and nutmeg to taste. Add cooked, drained vegetables, heat through, and check seasoning. If the sauce is poured over the whole loaf, sprinkle some of the parsley on top and the rest on the vegetables; otherwise, sprinkle it all on the vegetables.

For potatoes: Boil 4 to 8 medium potatoes in their skins. Cool, peel, cut in half, and add to the sauce. Place over low flame to heat through.

For onions: Peel 8 to 16 small white onions, allowing 2 to 4 per person, depending on the size. (Peeling can be facilitated by dropping the unpeeled onions into a pot of boiling water and leaving them for 5 to 10 seconds for the skins to loosen. Drain and run cold water over them, then cut a small piece off each end and slip the skins off.) Cut a small cross in the root end to help keep them from separating during cooking. Cook in a heavy, lidded saucepan or flameproof casserole, with about an inch of water in the bottom, 2 tablespoons of butter, and salt and pepper. Shake the pan occasionally, and cook until onions are just tender. Drain and add to the cream sauce. Heat through over low flame.

For celery: Trim 1 bunch of celery, discarding leafy tops. Separate stalks, wash, and scrape outside stalks if necessary to remove strings. Cut stalks into 2-inch pieces, and split the wide ends to make the pieces more or less uniform in size. Cook in a heavy, lidded saucepan or casserole, with 1½ cups water, 2 tablespoons butter, ½ teaspoon salt (or to taste), and a sprinkle of black pepper. Bring to a boil, cover, and cook over low heat until celery is just tender, about 20 minutes. Shake the pan occasionally. Drain and add to the cream sauce, and heat through over low heat. One bunch of celery serves 4 to 6.

Scalloped Potatoes

    4 cups potatoes, in $\frac{1}{16}$-inch slices
    1 medium onion, thinly sliced
  1–2 tablespoons flour
  3–4 tablespoons butter
     Salt, pepper, thyme
1½–2 cups hot milk

Rinse the potato slices until the water is clear. Dry on a clean kitchen towel. Divide the potatoes in three parts and the onions in two parts. Put a layer of potatoes in the bottom of a buttered casserole and cover with half the onions. Sprinkle with flour, dot with butter, and sprinkle with salt, pepper, and a pinch of thyme. Do the same with another layer of potatoes and onions. Top with the rest of the potatoes, and pour in hot milk to come halfway to the top of the potatoes. Sprinkle with salt, pepper, and a pinch of thyme, and dot with butter. Bake, uncovered, in a preheated 350° oven for 1 hour, or until potatoes are tender and brown in spots on the top. Serves 4.

Pommes Anna

6 baking potatoes
6 ounces butter (1½ sticks), more if needed
  Salt and freshly ground black pepper, to taste

  Parsley or watercress to garnish

Peel the potatoes and slice them into the thinnest possible rounds. There are gadgets for this, including the slicing section of an all-purpose grater. If you have to do it by hand, try for $\frac{1}{16}$-inch slices, as uniform as possible. Drop the slices into a bowl of cold water as you go along. The potatoes are to be arranged on the bottom of the cooking utensil with a capacity of 2 or 2½ quarts and slightly up the sides, cooked in butter until they are golden and crisp on the bottom and then inverted onto a platter, so the pan used needs some consideration. It should be lidded and ovenproof, and as non-stick as possible. A silicone-coated casserole would be excellent, or a well-seasoned iron frying pan, with a lid and ovenproof handle. Next best would be Pyrex or enameled ironware. (Pyrex has the advantage of allowing you to see how brown the potatoes are getting.)

With 2 to 3 tablespoons of the butter at room temperature, generously butter the pan. Melt the rest of the butter. Rinse the potatoes and dry them quickly between paper towels. Spread a layer of overlapping slices on the bottom of the pan and up the sides. Sprinkle with salt and pepper and pour some melted butter on top. Continue to make layers until all the potatoes are used up, salting, peppering, and pouring butter over each layer. If you run out of butter for the top layer, dot with a little more butter. Cover with a piece of waxed paper cut to fit, and the lid. Place in a preheated 400° oven for 40 to 60 minutes, until the butter is bubbling around the edges, the potatoes are tender, and the edges are crisp and brown. Loosen around the edge with a spatula, pour off excess butter (you may reserve it for other uses), and discard waxed paper. Place a warm platter over the pan and invert, to turn the potatoes out to show the beautiful brown crust. Garnish with parsley or watercress. Serves 4 to 6.

Hot Potato Salad

6 tablespoons oil
2 tablespoons vinegar
½ teaspoon salt, or to taste
¼ teaspoon pepper
1 teaspoon Dijon mustard

¼ cup chopped scallions, with tops
4 cups sliced, cooked potatoes
2 tablespoons finely chopped fresh parsley

Heat the oil, vinegar, salt, pepper, and mustard in a shallow saucepan or skillet. Add the scallions, potatoes, and parsley. Stir carefully to coat with the hot dressing. Cover for a minute or two, just to heat through, check seasoning, and serve immediately. (To make a cold version, cool and add 2 to 3 tablespoons of mayonnaise and 2 additional tablespoons of freshly chopped parsley.) Serves 4 to 6.

Lemon Rice

2 tablespoons butter
2 tablespoons oil
1 teaspoon salt
1 teaspoon mustard seeds
2 teaspoons turmeric
3 cups cooked rice
   Juice of 1 lemon, strained

¼ cup seedless yellow raisins (optional)

Heat the butter and oil on low heat, and add the seasonings. Stir and cook on the low heat until the mustard seeds jump. Add the rice and stir until all is blended and heated through. Add the lemon juice and mix again. If the rice has been chilled, it might be well to use the top part of a double boiler from the start, putting it over hot water to heat through when everything is mixed. Serves 4 to 6.

If desired, raisins can be added. Pour boiling water over the raisins and allow to stand for 10 minutes. Drain and stir into the rice mixture at the end.

A bowl of plain yogurt can be served separately, as a sauce for the rice or the meat dish.

Risotto

  1 tablespoon butter
  1 tablespoon oil
1½ cups uncooked rice
  1 medium onion, finely chopped

  3 cups canned chicken broth (13¾-ounce size)
½–1 teaspoon saffron threads, crumbled
    Salt and pepper (optional)

  2 tablespoons butter
¼–½ cup grated Parmesan cheese

Heat the butter and oil in a heavy, lidded saucepan or casserole. Add the rice and onion and cook slowly until the onion is transparent and the rice opaque and both are golden but not brown. Remove from the heat.

In another saucepan, bring the chicken broth to a boil with the saffron, and add to the rice and onion. Stir just once, put back on the heat, and bring to a boil. Turn heat down, cover tightly, and cook over a low flame for 20 to 25 minutes, or until the liquid is absorbed and the rice is tender. Fluff with a fork and check seasoning; salt and pepper may be needed if there is not enough taste in the broth.

Stir in the butter and the Parmesan cheese, or serve the cheese in a side dish, to be sprinkled on individual servings. Serves 6.

Rice Pilaf with Almonds

    1 tablespoon butter
    1 tablespoon oil
 1½ cups uncooked rice
    1 medium onion, finely chopped
  ⅓ cup coarsely chopped almonds

    3 cups canned beef broth (13¾-ounce size)
    1 teaspoon turmeric
       Salt and pepper (optional)

    2 tablespoons butter
  ⅓ cup yellow raisins (optional)

Heat the butter and oil in a heavy, lidded saucepan or casserole.
Add the rice, onion, and almonds and cook slowly until the onion is
transparent, the rice is opaque, and the almonds are golden, but
nothing is brown. Remove from the heat.

In another saucepan, bring the beef broth to a boil with the
turmeric, and add to the rice mixture. Stir just once, put back on
the heat, and bring to a boil. Turn heat down, cover tightly, and
cook over a low flame for 20 to 25 minutes, or until liquid is absorbed and rice is tender. Fluff with a fork and check seasoning;
salt and pepper may be needed if there is not enough taste in the
broth.

Stir in the butter. If you like yellow raisins in your pilaf, pour
boiling water over the raisins and allow to stand for 10 minutes.
Drain and stir into the rice at the end. Serves 6.

Spaghetti with Garlic Sauce

1 pound spaghetti

1 cup olive oil
4 cloves garlic
½ teaspoon salt
¼ teaspoon freshly ground black pepper

½ cup finely chopped parsley

Cook spaghetti according to package directions, using minimum time.

To make sauce, heat olive oil in a small saucepan, add garlic cloves, flattened with the flat of a big knife, salt, and pepper. Let it all steep, without letting the garlic brown, for 2 to 3 minutes. Discard the garlic and toss the sauce with the spaghetti and parsley. Serves 6 as a side dish.

Celery in Egg and Lemon Sauce

2 tablespoons butter
1 medium onion, finely chopped
1½ cups chicken broth, canned
    Salt and pepper
1 bunch celery

3 egg yolks
    Juice of 1 lemon, strained

In a heavy, lidded saucepan or casserole, large enough to accommodate the celery, melt the butter and cook the onion until it is soft but not brown. Add the chicken broth, and salt and pepper to taste (some chicken broths are more salty than others). Trim the celery, discarding leafy tops, separate the stalks, wash, and cut into 2-inch pieces. If the outside stalks are huge, they will need scraping to remove strings, and they can be split lengthwise. Add the celery to the broth and onion, bring to a simmer, cover, and cook for 15 to 20 minutes, or until just tender. Remove from the heat.

Beat the egg yolks and lemon juice together in a small bowl, add a little of the hot broth, and stir into the celery. Check seasoning, cover, and allow to stand for 5 minutes to thicken slightly. Do not reheat. To prepare ahead, cook celery as above and add the egg and lemon at serving time. Serves 4 to 6.

Five-Minute Carrots

    4 cups coarsely shredded carrots
    3 tablespoons water
    4 tablespoons butter
  ½ teaspoon salt or more, to taste
  ¼ teaspoon pepper
  ¼ teaspoon ground ginger

Combine all ingredients in a heavy, lidded saucepan or casserole. Bring to a simmer, cover, and cook 5 minutes, or until tender. Serves 6 to 8.

Ratatouille

This famous Mediterranean eggplant dish is an excellent accompaniment, hot or cold, for pâtés and meat loaves. It is hard to make a small quantity, by the time all those vegetables go in, but leftovers keep for several days in the refrigerator. The proportion of vegetables can vary, as long as you start with plenty of onions and garlic.

  2 tablespoons olive oil
  2 medium onions, coarsely chopped
  1 large green pepper, coarsely chopped
  2 cloves garlic, minced
  ¼ cup finely chopped fresh parsley

1 one-pound can Italian tomatoes
½ teaspoon salt
¼ teaspoon pepper
1 teaspoon oregano
½ teaspoon basil
1 bay leaf

1 medium eggplant
1 medium zucchini
2 tablespoons olive oil or more, as needed
  Salt and pepper to taste

Heat 2 tablespoons olive oil in a large, heavy, lidded skillet, prefer-ably enameled ironware, or a wide, shallow, flameproof casserole. Add the onions, green pepper, and garlic. Cook slowly until the onions are limp and transparent. Add the parsley, tomatoes, and seasonings. Bring to a boil, and turn down to the merest simmer.

Wash the eggplant, trim the ends, and cut into 1-inch cubes, leav-ing the skin on. Wash and lightly scrape the zucchini, cut off the ends, and cut in ½-inch slices. In another skillet, heat 2 tablespoons olive oil and quickly, over high heat, sauté the eggplant and zuc-chini, a few pieces at a time, until they start to show tiny specks of brown here and there. Use more oil as needed; eggplant soaks it up. Sprinkle with salt and pepper as they cook, and add to the simmer-ing tomato mixture as they are done. Stir and check seasoning, adding more salt, pepper, or herbs in small quantities, to taste. Partially cover and cook over very low heat for about 45 minutes, or until eggplant and zucchini are tender but not mushy. Stir oc-casionally during cooking. Can be served hot or cold. Serves 6 or more.

SALADS

Grated Carrot Salad

  2 cups finely shredded carrots
½ green pepper, finely chopped
  1 tablespoon minced shallots *or* 2 tablespoons finely chopped
    scallions with tops
  2 tablespoons finely chopped fresh parsley
½ recipe for French Dressing* (page 221), with a pinch of
    sugar added

Combine ingredients and serve on a bed of Boston lettuce or surrounded by watercress. Serves 4.

Orange and Cucumber Salad

  4 small navel oranges, peeled (leaving no white) and thinly sliced
  1 medium cucumber, scored with a fork and thinly sliced
¼ cup finely chopped scallions with green tops
  1 small Boston lettuce, washed, dried, and broken up
  1 recipe for French Dressing* (page 221)

Pour dressing over salad ingredients a few minutes before serving and toss just at serving time. Serves 6 to 8.

Sweet-Sour Cucumbers

2 medium cucumbers
Salted water to cover (½ teaspoon salt per cup)

⅔ cup cider vinegar
½ cup water
½ teaspoon salt
2 tablespoons sugar
¼ teaspoon pepper
1 tablespoon chopped fresh dill *or* 1 teaspoon dried dill

Scrub the cucumbers and cut off the ends but do not peel them. Score with a fork, and slice very thin. Cover with salted water and let them stand for an hour in the refrigerator.

Pour off the salted water and add the mixture of vinegar, water, salt, sugar, pepper, and dill. Chill for 2 or 3 hours, stirring occasionally. Serve in small portions—it is more a relish than a salad.

Salade Niçoise au Riz (with Rice)

Although not essential, Italian rice is good for this hearty salad, the kernels separate and rather firm. One cup of uncooked rice makes about 3 cups cooked, so this recipe makes quite a lot. (The amount of dressing is generous, too—about ¾ of a cup; you may not need that much, but the rice does absorb some.) The tuna fish is optional, and the anchovies can be cut down, depending on how the salad is to be used. To have the salad with a pâté, it should have no tuna fish and less anchovy. Used as a separate dish for a buffet, it can have all its wonders, and it would also be good that way to follow a pâté, as a separate course.

  3 medium tomatoes, chopped
  1 medium green pepper, finely chopped or in thin strips
  1 small red onion, finely chopped or in thin slices
  3 hard-cooked eggs, sliced
  1 two-ounce can anchovy fillets, drained and chopped
10 pitted black olives
10 pitted green olives
  1 6½- or 7-ounce can tuna fish, drained and flaked (optional)
  2 tablespoons capers, drained, *or* 2 small sour gherkins, chopped
  ¼ cup finely chopped fresh parsley

French Dressing:
  3 tablespoons wine vinegar
  ½ teaspoon Dijon mustard
  ¼ teaspoon salt, or to taste
  ¼ teaspoon freshly ground black pepper
  9 tablespoons olive oil, *or* part olive oil and part vegetable oil

3 cups cooked rice, chilled

Mix the other ingredients with ½ cup French Dressing and carefully stir in the rice. Add more dressing to taste. Serves 6 to 8.

Celery Root Rémoulade

2 medium celery knobs (celeriac), well pared
¾ cup mayonnaise
2 teaspoons Dijon mustard
   Lemon juice
   Freshly ground black pepper

Using a very sharp knife, cut the celery knobs into ¹⁄₁₆-inch slices. Cut the slices into the smallest possible strips. Mix the mayonnaise and mustard together and add lemon juice to taste. Combine the julienne of celery knobs with the mayonnaise mixture, add a grating of black pepper, and refrigerate until serving time. Serves 4 to 6.

COLD SAUCES

Sour Cream and Dill Sauce (for Cucumbers)

    1 cup sour cream
    1 tablespoon fresh dill or chives *or* 1 teaspoon dried dill
    ¼ teaspoon salt
    ¼ teaspoon white pepper
    1 teaspoon lemon juice

To make the sauce alone, mix ingredients together, check seasoning, and add more dill, salt, pepper, or lemon juice to taste. To serve with cucumbers, peel and halve two medium cucumbers lengthwise. Scoop out seeds and discard. Cut cucumbers across in ½-inch pieces and mix with sauce. Radishes may be substituted for one of the cucumbers. Serves 4 to 6.

French Dressing

⅛ teaspoon freshly ground black pepper
½ teaspoon Dijon mustard, *or* ⅛ teaspoon dry mustard
⅛–¼ teaspoon salt (to taste)
2 tablespoons wine or cider vinegar
6 tablespoons olive oil, salad oil, or a mixture of both

Mix pepper, mustard, and the minimum amount of salt with the vinegar. Beat in the oil and taste, adding more salt as desired. Makes about ½ cup.

Cumberland Sauce

1 tablespoon minced shallots *or* white part of scallions
Rind of 1 lemon and 1 orange (no white), in fine strips
Juice of ½ lemon and 1 orange
¾ cup red currant jelly, melted
¾ cup Port
1 teaspoon Dijon mustard
Pinch each cayenne pepper and ground ginger

Put the shallots (or scallions) and the orange and lemon rind in a saucepan with the fruit juice. Simmer for 10 minutes. Add the melted jelly and Port, and stir in the mustard, cayenne pepper, and ginger. Mix well and bring back to a simmer, stirring constantly.

Cool to room temperature. We like to serve the sauce strained for a pâté and unstrained for game, chicken, tongue, or ham. This recipe makes about 1½ cups, enough for about 30 servings.

Horseradish Sauce

½ cup heavy cream
¼ teaspoon salt, or to taste
 Pinch of pepper
2–3 tablespoons horseradish

Whip the cream, add the salt and pepper, and fold in the horseradish. Makes about 1 cup.

Sour cream can also be used for this sauce. Use 1 cup sour cream instead of the heavy cream; stir in salt, pepper, and horseradish to taste.

Vinaigrette Dressing

⅛–¼ teaspoon salt, or to taste
 ⅛ teaspoon freshly ground black pepper
 1 teaspoon Dijon mustard *or* ¼ teaspoon dry mustard
 1 tablespoon vinegar
 3 tablespoons olive oil or salad oil
 2 tablespoons minced shallots *or* scallions, green part included
 2 tablespoons finely chopped fresh parsley

Mix the salt, pepper, and mustard with the vinegar. Beat in the oil and stir in the vegetables. Start with the minimum amount of salt, and then taste after everything else has been added and adjust at that point. Makes about ½ cup.

Green Sauce

Double the preceding Vinaigrette recipe, add about ¾ cup fresh basil leaves, and whirl in the blender. This makes a marvelous dip for cold shrimp or crisp raw vegetables and a fine sauce for tomatoes. When you check the seasoning, remember that all these things can stand quite a strong sauce. Makes about 1 cup.

HOT SAUCES

Madeira Sauce

    3 tablespoons butter
    3 tablespoons minced shallots *or* onion
    2 tablespoons flour
    ⅓ cup Madeira
    1 can ready-to-use beef broth (13¾-ounce size)

In a small saucepan melt the butter, add the shallots or onion, and cook over low heat until they are soft but not brown. Stir in the flour, remove from the heat, and add the Madeira and broth, stirring until smooth. Bring to a boil, stirring, and cook over medium heat, to boil without boiling over, for 20 to 30 minutes, stirring occasionally, until sauce has reduced to 1½ cups.

Sour Cream Sauce

    1 cup sour cream
    2 tablespoons flour
    1 cup beef broth

¼ teaspoon white pepper
½ teaspoon salt, or to taste
2 tablespoons Amontillado Sherry

Stir sour cream and flour together in a saucepan. Gradually stir in beef broth and cook over low flame, stirring constantly, until bubbling and thickened. Add salt, pepper, and Sherry. Makes about 2 cups.

Mushroom Sauce

Add ½ to ¾ pound sautéed fresh mushrooms to Sour Cream Sauce or Madeira Sauce.

Tomato Sauce with Horseradish

2 cloves garlic, minced
4 teaspoons olive oil
1 one-pound can tomatoes, with juice
2 tablespoons tomato paste
1 can beef broth (13¾-ounce size)
¼ teaspoon freshly ground black pepper
½ teaspoon salt, or to taste
1 bay leaf
2 tablespoons horseradish, or to taste

Cook the garlic very briefly in the oil, not long enough to brown. Break up the tomatoes with a fork or fingers and add, all at once, to the garlic and oil. Mix in the tomato paste. Add the broth, pepper, salt, and bay leaf. Simmer, partially covered, for 1¼ hours. Stir in horseradish and serve. Makes about 1½ cups.

Creamy Mustard Sauce

2 tablespoons butter
2 tablespoons minced onion
2 tablespoons flour
4 teaspoons Dijon mustard, or more to taste
2 cups milk
¼ teaspoon salt, or to taste
¼ teaspoon white pepper

Cook the butter and onion together until the onion is soft but not brown. Mix in the flour and remove from the heat. Stir in the mustard to make a smooth paste. Gradually add the milk, and stir until smooth. Bring to a boil over low heat, stirring constantly. Add salt and pepper and continue to cook and stir for 2 or 3 minutes, until sauce has thickened. Check and adjust seasoning. Makes 2 cups.

WINE PUNCHES

Champagnes and sparkling wines of all sorts are good with pâtés, particularly when there is a taste of ham or smokiness. The Rhineland wines from the Riesling grape are almost too flowery for all but the saltiest and smokiest of pâtés. All these wines, however, make an excellent punch to serve by the pitcher at lunch or on the buffet.

Ice
2–4 ounces of Triple Sec or other sweet liqueur
  2 lemons, juice and peel
  1 orange, juice and peel
  1 bottle soda
  2 bottles Champagne or lesser sparkling wine
    Berries or peaches, fresh or frozen (optional)

Be sure that the wine and soda are well chilled. In a pitcher or bowl place a block of ice or two trays of ice, frozen without the cube dividers. Add the liqueur and fruits, the soda and sparkling wine. The peel is enough garnish, but berries or peaches, fresh or frozen, can be added. Serves 4 to 6.

Variations

When a tarter punch is wanted, use Cognac instead of a sweet liqueur, grapes for garnish.

This punch can be made with white wine, a dry Burgundy, or a flowery Alsatian or Rhine wine instead of Champagne, in which case, vodka or gin might be used as the spirit. For serving with pâtés, the drier versions are best, omitting the orange and substituting long slivers of cucumber and its peel for one or both of the lemons.

Red Wine Punch

Inexpensive red wines, particularly jug wines sold by the gallon or half gallon, often taste better when made into a punch, like the Spanish Sangría. Too many additions often confuse the taste, and perhaps the simplest version is best.

    Ice
2–4 ounces of Cognac or other good brandy
  1 lemon, juice and peel
  1 orange, sliced
  1 bottle soda
  1 bottle dry red wine

Both wine and soda should be chilled

Put in a pitcher or bowl a block of ice or two trays of ice, frozen without the cube dividers. Add the Cognac and the fruit, the soda and the wine. The peel and slices provide enough garnish. Serves 4 to 6.

Variations

Calvados, Bourbon, or vodka can replace the brandy. Tea can be used to replace half the soda. A second bottle of wine can be added for a more pronounced taste of wine.

INDEX

PÂTÉ MAISON...

VEAL & PORK LOAF IN ASPIC...

SAUMON AU RIZ EN CROÛTE...

SALMON LOAF IN PASTRY...

MATAMBRE...

STUFFED ROLLED BEEF LOAF...

MOUSSE DE JAMBON...

HAM MOUSSE...

FISKEPUDDING...

FISH LOAF WITH SHRIMP SAUCE...

GALANTINE DE CANARD...

BONED STUFFED DUCK...